Instructor's Resource Manual
with Core Concept Video Instructor's Guide
to accompany
Liberty, Equality, Power
A History of the American People
Second Edition

Volume I: To 1877

John M. Murrin
Paul E. Johnson
James M. McPherson
Gary Gerstle
Emily S. Rosenberg
Norman L. Rosenberg

Prepared by
Peter Field
Jeffery Roberts
Larry Whiteaker
Tennessee Technical University

Harcourt Brace College Publishers

Fort Worth   Philadelphia   San Diego   New York   Orlando   Austin   San Antonio
Toronto   Montreal   London   Sydney   Tokyo

Cover Image: Albert Bierstadt, "The Oregon Trail," 1869. The Butler Institute of American Art, Youngstown, Ohio.

ISBN: 0–15–508103–9

Address for Editorial Correspondence:
Harcourt Brace College Publishers, 301 Commerce Street, Suite 3700, Fort Worth, TX 76102

Address for Orders:
Harcourt Brace & Company, 6277 Sea Harbor Drive, Orlando, FL 32887-6777. 1-800-782-4479

Web site address: http://www.hbcollege.com

Harcourt Brace College Publishers may provide complimentary instructional aids and supplements or supplement packages to those adopters qualified under our adoption policy. Please contact your sales representative for more information. If as an adopter or potential user you receive supplements you do not need, please return them to your sales representative or send them to:

Attention: Returns Department, Troy Warehouse, 465 South Lincoln Drive, Troy, MO 63379

Printed in the United States of America

8 9 0 1 2 3 4 5 6 7   023   10 9 8 7 6 5 4 3 2 1

Preface

This *Instructor's Resource Manual* is intended as a teaching supplement. It is designed to be used in conjunction with Harcourt Brace's *Liberty, Equality, Power: A History of the American People*, Second Edition. We have attempted to construct a work reflecting the innovative thematic approach taken by the textbook's authors. Accordingly, with the exception of the "Liberty, Equality, Power: A Thematic Braid" section, instructors will find little particularly novel here. Rather, we hope that instructors will discover a resource to facilitate the classroom use of an extremely balanced and insightful narrative of the American experience.

The authors of the *Instructor's Resource Manual* are seasoned teachers of American history. We assume that instructors adopting the *Liberty, Equality, Power* text either have completed, or are in the process of completing, advanced work in American history. The *Instructor's Resource Manual* certainly is not intended to instruct instructors or teach teachers. Its purpose is to serve as a supplement only. Ideally, it will assist instructors in planning their classes, in offering quality assignments based closely on the textbook material, and, perhaps most importantly, in refreshing themselves on the precise material contained in the text itself. We feel confident that instructors consulting the *Instructor's Resource Manual* will readily know what to expect their students to understand from their textbook assignments.

For convenience, the *Instructor's Resource Manual* consists of separate sections including the following: a chapter summary, a chronology, a list of identification terms, geography objectives, suggested thematic topics for classroom discussion and written assignments, lecture outlines (new to the Second Edition), and a brief guide to video resources to augment classroom lectures.

Finally, a word is in order concerning the "Thematic Braid" portion of the manual. In this section, we have attempted to outline in brief what helps to make *Liberty, Equality, Power: A History of the American People* an exceptional college history textbook—its thematic consistency. The "Thematic Braid" portion of the *Instructor's Resource Manual* encapsulates the overall themes of each chapter, summarizing the textbook's interweaving of the themes of liberty, equality, and power.

It is impossible to assemble a guide to meet all instructors' needs. Teachers are encouraged to pick and choose from among the numerous parts as they see fit. By their doing so, we hope that instructors will find this work a helpful resource for teaching with *Liberty, Equality, Power: A History of the American People*, Second Edition.

—PSF, JJR, LHW

Contents

Preface   iii

Chapter 1
When Old Worlds Collide: Contact, Conquest, Catastrophe   1

Chapter 2
The Challenge to Spain and the Settlement of North America   7

Chapter 3
England Discovers Its Colonies: Empire, Liberty, and Expansion   15

Chapter 4
Provincial America and the Struggle for a Continent   21

Chapter 5
Reform, Resistance, Revolution   29

Chapter 6
The Revolutionary Republic   37

Chapter 7
The Democratic Republic, 1790–1820   45

Chapter 8
Completing the Revolution, 1789–1815   59

Chapter 9
The Market Revolution, 1815–1860   67

Chapter 10
Toward an American Culture   73

Chapter 11
Society, Culture, and Politics, 1820s–1840s   79

Chapter 12
Jacksonian Democracy   85

Chapter 13
Manifest Destiny: An Empire for Liberty—or Slavery?   91

Chapter 14
The Gathering Tempest, 1853–1860   97

Chapter 15
Secession and Civil War, 1860–1862   103

Chapter 16
A New Birth of Freedom, 1862–1865   111

Chapter 17
Reconstruction, 1863–1877   121

Core Concept Video Instructor's Guide   129

Chapter 1
When Old Worlds Collide:
Contact, Conquest, Catastrophe

CHAPTER SUMMARY

Most textbooks assume that "real" history did not begin in the Americas until after Europeans arrived in 1492. This chapter shows that a varied and complex past shaped Indian cultures and profoundly conditioned their response to the arrival of Europeans. Religion, gender relations, warfare, and trade differed enormously and created different value systems on the two sides of the Atlantic.

Christopher Columbus was not the first person to travel between the Eastern and Western Hemispheres. Far from it. The first inhabitants of the Americas traversed the Beringia land bridge from Asia. Norsemen from Scandinavia sailed west across the North Atlantic long before 1492. The significance of Columbus's feat proved to be the permanent connection he inaugurated between the peoples, flora, and fauna of both sides of the Atlantic that had been separated for over 5,000 years. Called by historians the Columbian Exchange, this linking of East and West proved revolutionary for everyone and everything in Europe, Africa, North America, and South America.

No group suffered more from the Columbian Exchange than the Amerindian peoples, who had no immunity to smallpox and the other microparasites of the Europeans. The Inca and Aztec civilizations, so remarkable for their urban societies, native art and animistic religion, were no match for the armored and mounted Spanish forces, especially while suffering under the all-but-incalculable strain of virgin-soil epidemics. Within a few decades the great Amerindian civilizations all but disappeared. While Spanish and other European missionaries sought to do the work of God, their efforts failed to alter the brutal, inhuman treatment of the indigenous peoples of the Americas.

As a result of their exploration and conquest, Europeans—Iberians in particular—transformed themselves from a relatively weak and isolated region into the world's most dominant civilization. In spite of brutal indifference to human life, huge bureaucratic inefficiency, and frequent internecine wars, the Europeans rode their warships in search of gold, glory, and the Gospel. In doing so, they marched toward world domination.

LIBERTY, EQUALITY, POWER: A THEMATIC BRAID

Columbus's voyage and those that followed were fueled in no small measure by the European desire for power, particularly the power to dominate the eastern trade. The European notions of equality, like those of the scattered civilizations of the globe, proved exceedingly limited. Indeed, the world in 1500 was one so full of hierarchy and inequality that virtually no one proposed, or even imagined, a society in which "all men are created equal." Indeed, the primary premise of virtually all peoples proved to be the distinction between "us and them," a distinction that contributed to the ruthless and barbaric nature of the Columbian Exchange.

Cultural differences contributed to Europeans' savage conquest of the Amerindian peoples. Missionary work and mass conversions failed to ameliorate European domination and at times even fostered it. Far more important proved to be Europe's insatiable appetite for glory and wealth. The discovery of the vast and, for the most part, indefensible riches of the new world brought out the most aggressive traits in the conquerors. The dominant theme of European world conquest proved to be the search for wealth and power.

IDENTIFICATIONS

Beringia	Clovis tip
Norseman	Vinland
Inuit	Black Death
Johann Gutenberg	caravel
Islam	Prince Henry
Cape of Good Hope	Isabella and Ferdinand
Treaty of Tordesillas	Christopher Columbus
Ponce de León	Tenochtitlán
Cahokia	kiva
Anasazi	Moundbuilders
Aztec	Maya
Hernán Cortés	slash and burn
Moctezuma	Inca
conquistadores	encomienda
haciendas	de Soto
Cabeza de Vaca	de Coronado
Francisco Pizarro	Council of the Indies
smallpox	Columbian Exchange
Elmina	Fray Bartholomé de Las Casas
Jesuits	Franciscans
Royal Order for New Discoveries	Brazil

CHRONOLOGY

50,000–10,000 B.C.	Migrations over Beringia into the Americas.
9000–8000 B.C.	Clovis tip hunter-gatherer culture spreads throughout North America.
3400 B.C. –A.D. 700	Louisiana moundbuilders' culture extends through southeastern North America.
500 B.C. –A.D. 400	Adena-Hopewell moundbuilders flourish in the Ohio Valley.
A.D. 900–1200	Anasazi culture expands through southwest North America.
1001–1014	Leif Erikson leads three voyages to North America.
1347–1351	Bubonic plague, the "Black Death," decimates one third of the European population.
1400–1450	Aztec and Incan conquests of, respectively, Mesoamerica and Andean South America.
1434	Gil Eannes rounds Cape Bojador and returns safely to Portugal.
1430s	Johann Gutenberg invents movable-type printing press.
1440s	Portuguese enter the African slave trade.

1492	Spanish victory at Granada results in overthrow of last outpost of Islam in Iberia.
	Christopher Columbus's first voyage to the Western Hemisphere.
1494	Treaty of Tordesillas divides non-Christian world between Spanish and Portuguese.
1497–1499	Vasco da Gama sails to India and back.
1500	Portugese discover Brazil.
1501	First slaves carried from Africa to the Americas.
1519	Ferdinand Magellan sets sail from Seville, Spain, beginning the first circumnavigation of the globe.
	Hernán Cortés begins conquest of Aztecs.
1528–1536	Cabeza de Vaca travels overland from Florida to Mexico.
1531–1532	Francisco Pizarro leads expedition against the Inca.
1539–1543	Hernando de Soto's expedition through the southeastern part of North America.
1540–1542	Francisco de Coronado's expedition through the southwestern part of North America.
1540s	Spanish assume control over the silver mines at Potosí.
1570–1571	First Spanish Jesuit mission in Chesapeake Bay.
1580	Philip II unites the Spanish and Portuguese empires.

THEMATIC TOPICS FOR ENRICHMENT

1. What elements of world geography did Columbus possess knowledge of right before setting out in 1492? What elements did he have wrong?

2. Give examples of the biological, environmental, and cultural consequences of the Columbian Exchange.

3. Discuss the use of the word *catastrophe* to describe the results of "Old Worlds Colliding" in the fifteenth and sixteenth centuries.

4. List the merits and detractions of the following terms used to identify the peoples of the Americas: Indians, Americans, Amerindians, Natives, Native Americans.

5. Contrast the various peoples who came to the Americas before 1600. Why did some stay, but others did not?

6. Explain the statement: "In 1400, Europe stood at the edge, not the center, of world commerce."

7. Discuss the rise of Portugal as a seaborne empire in the fifteenth century. Why does the text call it an "unlikely pioneer?"

8. What were Columbus's motives in 1492, and what were those of the Spaniards who followed him to the Americas?

9. How did the Spanish conquistadores manage to subdue the great Amerindian civilizations of the Aztecs and the Inca?

10. Contrast the idealism and chauvinism of the missionary efforts in the Western Hemisphere.

GEOGRAPHY OBJECTIVES

1. Find the location of the following civilizations on a map: Mali, Chinese, Ottoman, Western European, Amerindian (pp. 8, 39).

2. Trace the route of the Silk Road. Show how Columbus intended to sail west to establish a competing trade route (p. 8).

3. Sketch where the Beringia land bridge was located when revealed by the lowered sea level of the last Ice Age (p. 3).

4. Locate the Maya, Aztec, Inca, Anasazi, and eastern woodlands peoples on a map of the Americas (p. 35).

5. Find Greenland, Alaska, and Tierra del Fuego on a map of the Western Hemisphere (p. 39).

SUGGESTED ESSAY TOPICS

1. After 500 years, how has our evaluation of Columbus's voyages changed?

2. What advantages did Europeans have over other civilizations in 1500? What disadvantages did they turn to their ultimate benefit?

3. Create your own accounts of the conquest of the Aztec civilization from the contrasting points of view of Moctezuma and Cortés. In what ways can the conflict be described as a "cultural misunderstanding"?

4. What were the basic mechanisms of the slave trade? Assess the relationship of slavery and the conquest of the Western Hemisphere.

LECTURE OUTLINE

1. The story of the settlement of the Americas is only one part of a larger epic of **peoples in motion**, of which the Western Hemisphere was only one destination.
   a. The first immigrants traveled from **Beringia to the Americas** over the land bridge created during the last Ice Age.

   (Show Transparency 01-02: Map, Indian Settlement of America)

   b. Climatic changes led to the **great extinction** of the large mammals upon which the bands of hunters depended; extinction led to the **rise of agriculture** in the aftermath of the last Ice Age.
   c. Explorers from the west known as **Polynesians** settled **Hawaii** and other islands in the eastern Pacific Ocean.
   d. Peoples from the north, **Norsemen**, traveled from the upper reaches of Europe to North America long before Columbus's voyages.

2. **Europe in the fifteenth century** was just one part of a world that encompassed myriad complex and competing societies.
   a. For reasons that are not entirely clear, **China**, the world's most populous country and in many ways its most advanced, rejected any organized plan of **Overseas Expansion**.

b. One key theme of fifteenth-century expansion was the persistent competition of **Europe versus Islam**, which included the cultural **legacy of the Crusades** and bitter enmity.

c. Portugal was the **unlikely pioneer** of European expansion, as the nation of only several hundred thousand established a remarkable empire in Africa, India, and Asia; its experiences and instigation of the **Slave Trade** provided the rest of Europe with important **Early Lessons**.

(Show Transparency 01-03: Map, Africa and the Mediterranean in the Fifteenth Century)

d. Much larger and more populous than its neighbor, Spain followed closely on Portugal's heels and soon eclipsed it in the race for an Atlantic empire.

   i. Sailing under the Spanish flag, Christopher Columbus accidentally found the Americas.

(Show Transparency 01-04: Map, Columbus's First Voyage, 1492)

   ii. Spain quickly established an empire in the **Caribbean** in the aftermath of Columbus's expeditions.

3. The centuries before Columbus witnessed the **emergence of complex societies in the Americas**.

a. The **rise of sedentary cultures** occurred throughout the Americas.

   i. The **Andes** contained a number of **cycles of complex cultures**, culminating in the **Inca civilization**, which thrived on its ingenious methods of terrace agriculture.

   ii. **Mesoamerica** also featured successive cycles of complex cultures, including the **Aztecs and Tenochtitlán**, **North American moundbuilders**, and **urban cultures of southwest North America**.

(Show Transparency 01-05: Map, Ancient Mesoamerica)

4. 1492 marked the first permanent **contact**; shortly thereafter, **cultural misunderstandings**, particularly over issues of religion and gender, resulted in conflict and open warfare.

5. By the turn of the century, cultural misunderstandings resulted in **conquest and catastrophe**.

a. Hernán Cortés led a band of less than a thousand men in the **conquest of Mexico**, while little more than a decade later the **Pizarro brothers** brutally subdued the Incas in Peru.

b. **North American conquistadores and missionaries** soon spread out from the Caribbean, simultaneously spreading Christianity and establishing Spanish dominion.

(Show Transparency 01-06: Map, Principal Spanish Explorations of North America; and Transparency 01-07: Map, Spanish Missions in Florida and New Mexico, circa 1675)

6. Through the sixteenth century, the Spaniards erected a remarkable **Empire** while unleashing a **demographic catastrophe** on the Indians.

(Show Transparency 01-01: Aztec drawing, Ravages of Smallpox)

7. Spanish and other European seamen copied Portuguese activities in **Brazil**, creating the beginnings of a **global economy** based largely upon slave labor and staple crop production.

8. Historians have suggested many conflicting explanations for the various **patterns of conquest, submission, and resistance** in the century following Columbus's voyages.

American Album: Global Empire: The Aesthetics of Power

Conclusion: By accident, on October 12, 1492, Christopher Columbus found America. From then on, and for the next several hundred years, Europeans contested for domination of the Western Hemisphere. The costs were high, and the consequences for the peoples of Europe, Africa, and the Americas proved all but immeasurable. For the indigenous peoples of the Western Hemisphere, the consequences of contact proved catastrophic.

TEACHING RESOURCES

Vikings! is a nine-part series "through the legendary world" of the Norsemen, narrated by Magnus Magnusson. PBS Video (running time is about 60 minutes per tape).

Vikings in North America offers a briefer account of the early expeditions. A&E (50 minutes).

Surviving Columbus: The Story of the Pueblo People, tells "the other side of history—as viewed by America's Pueblo people." PBS Home Video (52 minutes).

The First Americans reviews likely migration across Beringia into the Americas and is based on meteorological and archeological evidence. Filmic Archives (53 minutes).

Mesa Verde National Park is an archeological exploration through this Colorado national park, featuring Robert H. Lister, one of the United States's foremost anthropologists of the Anasazi civilization. Holiday Video Library (60 minutes).

Ferdinand and Isabella tells the story of the Spanish monarchy in the age of Columbus. Filmic Archives (30 minutes).

Central America: The Burden of Time explores the ways the Aztecs and Mayans developed civilization isolated from the rest of the world. Filmic Archives (60 minutes).

The Search for Ancient Americans attempts to unlock the secrets of the American past through the examination of five archeological landmarks. Filmic Archives (58 minutes).

Cannibals! examines missionary tales of human sacrifice and consumption in light of European bias and the historical record. Were the tales of cannibalism fantasy or fact? Films for the Humanities (28 minutes).

The Shape of the World: Staking a Claim details the Spanish conquistadores as they wreaked havoc upon the Mesoamerican and South American civilizations. Filmic Archives (55 minutes).

Ten Who Dared: Francisco Pizarro recreates this Spaniard's dramatic expedition of discovery and conquest. BBC/Time–Life Video (52 minutes).

Mysteries of Peru: Enigma of the Ruins explores in detail the remarkable and sophisticated Inca civilization of the Andes. Filmic Archives (50 minutes).

Chapter 2
The Challenge to Spain and the Settlement of North America

CHAPTER SUMMARY

The tremendous booty the Spanish hauled back from the Americas inevitably led other European nations to challenge Spain in the New World. By the beginning of the seventeenth century, the Dutch, English, and French had staked their own claims to the Atlantic sea lanes, to the slave trade, and to lands in the Caribbean and in North America. Catholic New France and Protestant New Netherland and the fledgling English colonies joined New Spain as outposts of the European empire.

The societies that these European nations created in the Western Hemisphere differed greatly from one another. They at once reflected the demographic, economic, and cultural features of their parent countries and proved remarkably distinctive in their own right. Like the motives of the Spanish conquistadores and hidalgos, those of the later settlers varied greatly. The earliest navigators—Cabot, Verrazzano, and Hudson—proved predominantly to be adventurers and explorers, who, like Columbus, sought to gain quick riches through exploration and conquest. While many early settlers were impelled by the allure of great wealth and personal fame, others sought to come to the West for religious and political reasons. The Protestant Reformation shook many of Europe's oldest institutions. Powerful Protestant movements in France, the Netherlands, and England challenged Catholicism in Europe. Similarly, Protestants sought to overturn Catholic Spain's domination of the Western Hemisphere. Finding no great societies like the Aztec or Inca that could be plundered, France, England, and the Netherlands gained little from their explorations through the first decades of the seventeenth century.

The French colonization effort centered in the Saint Lawrence River valley, which had been explored by Jacques Cartier between 1534 and 1543. The inhabitants of New France established good relations with the indigenous tribes, with whom they engaged in a lucrative fur trade. In spite of numerous hardships, including rather small numbers, extremely harsh winters, and the frequent indifference of the French crown, the missionaries and fur traders managed to establish a stable and successful, if not thriving, outpost in North America by the 1660s.

The Dutch settlement of North America, orchestrated by the Dutch West India Company, proved similar to that of the French. Establishing New Netherland primarily in the Hudson River valley, the West India Company suffered from a lack of funds as well as a shortage of settlers. Even with the enticement of huge patroonships, the company simply could not attract enough settlers to become more than a trading entrepôt, with outposts on the island of Manhattan and at Fort Orange. Good relations with the Iroquois nation, a policy of toleration modeled on the home country, as well as the efforts of zealous Dutch Reformed churchmen, enabled the colony to grow gradually through the first half of the seventeenth century.

England's early attempts to rival the Spanish failed for the most part. Only after the defeat of the Spanish Armada in 1588 and the union of West Country experience and London capital did colonization of North America and the Caribbean become feasible.

The Virginia Company and the Massachusetts Bay Company, both joint–stock companies, and a small band of Protestant Separatists who landed at Plymouth in 1620 established the first permanent English colonies in North America. All three suffered from a lack of funds, harsh initial conditions, and strained relations with the Amerindian nations. Yet their experiences proved vastly different. The Puritan settlements in New England quickly developed into remarkably stable and secure colonies with a rapidly growing population and diverse economies. The Chesapeake colonies of Virginia and Maryland suffered from disease, warfare, and the boom-and-bust cycle of an economy based solely on tobacco production. Not until the middle of the seventeenth century did the Chesapeake colonies become a tolerably stable society of planters, indentured servants, and a growing number of African slaves.

After the restoration of the Stuart monarchy, England began a concerted effort to settle North America. Under Charles II, England founded several colonies. Charles made effective use of the colonies to help pay off debts, granting huge tracts of land, called proprietorships, in North America. By royal charter, Lord Ashley-Cooper established Carolina; the duke of York, the king's brother, transformed New Netherland into New York; Lords Carteret and Berkeley founded New Jersey; and William Penn created a Quaker refuge that the king called Pennsylvania.

In sum, then, the nations of northwestern Europe established a wide spectrum of settlements in the Americas. Although they differed greatly from one another, they were similar in the direct and enduring challenge they presented to Spanish dominance of the New World.

LIBERTY, EQUALITY, POWER: A THEMATIC BRAID

European competition and conflict formed the backdrop of New World settlement in the sixteenth and seventeenth centuries. Conflict in Europe over power, religion, and empire spread inevitably into the Atlantic frontier, where England, France, and the Netherlands challenged Iberian dominance. Like the Spanish and Portuguese before them, the English, French, and Dutch hungered for vast riches to plunder in the Americas. Unable to break Spain's domination of Central and South America, they were forced to resort to piracy, illicit trade on the periphery of New Spain, and eventually, colonization of North America. Flush with imperial success and with coffers teeming with bullion, the Spanish undermined their own position by squandering their newfound riches and undertaking ill-fated wars with their northern neighbors. As a result, with the defeat of the Spanish Armada in 1588, power in the Atlantic frontier began to shift toward the Dutch and the English.

The English, French, and Dutch colonies in North America evolved very differently from those of the Spanish. Just as the regimes of England and the Netherlands were far less autocratic than Spain's, so, too, were those of the English and Dutch colonies. For many reasons, New France, New Netherland, and the English colonies engendered a rudimentary type of frontier liberty and emerging economic opportunities without parallel in Europe. The lack of indigenous empires to conquer, better relations with native peoples, the relative weakness of imperial control, and the diversity of the initial settlers all contributed to a greater atmosphere of liberty in the North American settlements. In these new settlements, transplanted Europeans germinated a rough and still inarticulate sense of equality.

IDENTIFICATIONS

staple crop agriculture
New Netherland
Giovanni da Verrazzano
Martin Luther
Protestant Reformation
Jacques Cartier
Samuel de Champlain
Thirty Years' War
Dutch West India Company
Pierre Minuit
Dutch Reformed Church
Henry VIII, Elizabeth I, Mary I
John Hawkins and Francis Drake
Roanoke Island
London Company
Captain John Smith
Powhatan
Opechancanough
Headrights
House of Burgesses
George Calvert
Pilgrims
John Winthrop
joint-stock company
Anne Hutchinson
Massachusetts' Body of Liberties
West Indies
Pequot War
Oliver Cromwell
Restoration
James Harrington
Barbados
Anglo-Dutch Wars
Society of Friends

New France
Francis I
Magellan
Calvinism
northwest passage
Huguenots
Etienne Brûlé
Henry Hudson
Fort Orange
patroonship
John Cabot (Giavanni Cabato)
Church of England
Humphrey Gilbert
Spanish Armada
joint-stock company
Jamestown
Pocahontas
royal colony
indentures
proprietary colony
Toleration Act of 1649
Mayflower Compact
covenant theology
Puritanism
Roger Williams
Half-Way Covenant
John Cotton
Stuart Dynasty
New Model Army
John Locke
Fundamental Constitutions of Carolina
Royal African Company
George Fox
William Penn

CHRONOLOGY

1497	John Cabot reaches North America.
1517	Martin Luther posts Ninety-Five Theses on Wittenburg Church, inaugurating the Protestant Reformation.
1524	Giovanni Verrazzano explores the coast of North America.
1534–1543	Jacques Cartier explores the St. Lawrence valley.
1558	Accession of Queen Elizabeth I.

1560–1590s	English conquest of Ireland.
1585–1590	Walter Raleigh's three failed attempts to launch a colony off Virginia.
1588	Defeat of the Spanish Armada.
1602	Dutch East India Company chartered.
1603	James I becomes King of England.
1607	Virginia Company founds Jamestown.
1608	Samuel de Champlain founds Quebec.
1609	Henry Hudson sails into Hudson River valley.
1618–1648	Thirty Years' War.
1619	Virginia House of Burgesses created.
	First African slaves sold in British North America.
1620	Separatists found Plymouth Colony.
1622	Opechancanough attacks Virginia.
1626	Pierre Minuit buys Manhattan Island, establishing New Netherland colony.
1629	Puritans found Massachusetts Bay Colony.
1632	George Calvert founds Maryland.
1636	Harvard College founded.
1636–1638	Roger Williams and Anne Hutchinson found Rhode Island.
1637	New England settlers slaughter Pequot Indians.
1640–1649	First English Civil War.
1641	Massachusetts General Court issues Body of Liberties.
1643	New Netherland carries out the Pavonia Massacre.
1649	Maryland Act of Toleration.
1640s	The sugar revolution and the rise of slavery in Barbados.
1660–1688	Restoration Era.
1660	Charles II becomes King of England.
1660s	Royal African Company established.
1662	Half-Way Covenant.
1663	Louis XIV assumes direct control over New France.
1663–1665	Carolina colony established by Ashley-Cooper.
1664	Duke of York granted charter for New York colony.
1665	New Jersey charter.
1680–1681	William Penn founds Pennsylvania colony.

THEMATIC TOPICS FOR ENRICHMENT

1. Define the various "spiritual frontiers" in the Americas. How important was missionary work in the European settlements?

2. Assess the statement of King Francis I of France that only by occupying a distant land could one acquire a valid claim to it. In what ways was New France a successful colony, and in what ways was it a failure?

3. Describe life in the early Chesapeake Bay area.

4. Discuss the special problems of the New Netherland colony and its attempts to overcome them. Were they successful?

5. Evaluate the Dutch conviction that "frank acceptance of religious diversity might stimulate trade."

6. Compare the demographics of the several New World colonies. Why was the mortality rate in New England so much lower than in the Chesapeake?

7. What was the Massachusetts 1641 "Body of Liberties," and what precedents did it set?

8. What was the relationship betwen toleration and suppression of dissent in Puritan Massachusetts?

9. What were the chief differences between class and caste in the American colonies?

10. What was the Puritan Revolution of the 1640s, and what were its effects upon colonial development?

11. Explain the quote: "England discovered its colonies and their importance around 1650."

12. Give a brief overview of the founding of the Restoration Colonies. What do the authors mean by "Far more than New England or Virginia, the Restoration Colonies foreshadowed what the United States became in later centuries"?

13. Which British colonies were proprietorships? Who were the proprietors, and what did they hope to accomplish?

14. Discuss the significance of the Dutch roots of the New York colony.

15. Enumerate and discuss the unique social features of the Pennsylvania colony.

16. What were the causes and the consequences of Bacon's Rebellion in Virginia?

GEOGRAPHY OBJECTIVES

1. Find England, France, and the Netherlands on a map of Europe (p. 15).

2. Draw the triangular route of a Portuguese slave ship from Europe to Africa to Brazil and back to Portugal (p. 39).

3. Identify the following rivers in North America: Saint Lawrence, Charles, Hudson, Delaware, James (p. 58).

4. Find the Leeward Islands, Jamaica, Barbados, and Hispaniola in the Caribbean Sea (p. 64).

5. Compare the sailing routes from Spain and Portugal to the New World with those of England and the Netherlands (p. 15).

6. Compare the extent of British North American settlements before the Restoration with that at the turn of the eighteenth century (p. 88).

SUGGESTED ESSAY TOPICS

1. In what ways did the societies that Europeans created in America differ from one another? In what ways were they similar?

2. Explain the major differences between Catholicism and Protestantism (Calvinism, in particular).

3. How successful were colonists at duplicating the society of their parent cultures?

4. Assess the following statement: "New England proved an ideal model for how to build a colony, while Virginia proved an example of how not to establish one."

5. Discuss the role of religion in the founding of the European colonies in the Americas.

LECTURE OUTLINE

1. The **Protestant Reformation** in Europe provided one **challenge to Spain** and set the tenor for European conflict, based on religious differences.

2. **New France** comprised sparsely settled trading entrepôts primarily along the Saint Lawrence River, where the inhabitants suffered through the frigid winter in order to trade in furs.

   (Show Transparency 02-02: Map, New France and the Jesuit Missions)

   a. **Early French explorers** included da Verrazano and Cartier; they were sent abroad at the behest of King Francis I in an attempt to claim some of the Western Hemisphere for France.

   b. **New France under Louis XIV** remained an underpopulated outpost characterized **by missions and the fur trade**, but little else.

3. **The Dutch and Swedish settlements** of North America in the Hudson River and Delaware Bay were primarily trading outposts characterized by reasonably good relations with the Indian peoples.

   a. Sparsely populated **New Netherland** was essentially the dominion of The East and West India Companies, as the government of the Netherlands had few resources to devote to full-scale colonization of North America.

   b. New Netherland proved one of the first **pluralistic societies**, by necessity containing ethnic and religious diversity.

   c. **Swedish and English encroachments** on the Dutch led to conflict by the 1640s.

4. Increasing numbers of settlers, relative stability, and a growing economy helped to spark a **challenge to all empires from Elizabethan England**.

   a. When the strife of the **English Reformation** finally subsided with the accession of Queen Elizabeth and the permanent establishment of the Anglican Church, England could direct more of its resources to colonization.

   b. England benefited from its several **rehearsals for colonization** of North America.
      i. Before any full-scale colonization, the pirates **Hawkins and Drake** plundered the Spanish Main in search of gold and glory.
      ii. **Sir Humphrey Gilbert**, having brutally colonized **Ireland**, set his sights on establishing settlements in America.
      iii. **Walter Raleigh** attempted three successive settlements in the Chesapeake, including **Roanoke**, but was refused by the queen to lead his expeditions in person.

   (Show Transparency 02-03: Map, Roanoke Colony, 1584–1590)

c. The seventeenth century marked **the swarming of the English** in successive waves onto the North American shores in numbers unmatched by any other European nation.

(Show Transparency 02-01: brochure promoting Virginia colony; and Transparency 02-04: Map, Virginia Company Charter, 1606)

d. The first permanent English migrations went to **The Chesapeake and the West Indian Colonies**, where they suffered greatly from disease and Indian attacks.
   i. The first Chesapeake settlement turned into the **Jamestown Disaster** of 1607, when the colony ran out of food and the settlers suffered from devastating illnesses.
   ii. More attention by the Crown led to **reorganization, reform, and crisis** in the first decades of Virginia's history, culminating in the replacement of the Virginia Company's charter with royal control.
   iii. The **survival** and economic viability of the fledgling colony depended overwhelmingly on **tobacco** and the importation of white indentured **servants**.
   iv. Charles I granted Lord Baltimore the charter to **Maryland** in 1632.

   (Show Transparency 02-05: Map, Virginia and Maryland, circa 1675)

   v. A disproportion of men, short life expectancy, high rates of illegitimacy, and frequent remarriage among women characterized **Chesapeake family life**.
   vi. The **West Indies** produced labor-intensive staple crops that virtually guaranteed the **transition to slavery**.

   (Show Transparency 02-06: Map, Principal West Indian Colonies in the seventeenth century)

   vii. **The rise of slavery in North America** proved gradual, with few laws distinguishing between white and black until the eighteenth century.
e. Seeking relief from religious persecution, dissenters of all stripes dominated the settlement of the **New England colonies.**

   (Show Transparency 02-07: Map, New England in the 1640s)

   i. **The Pilgrims** fled Europe to establish **Plymouth** in 1620.
   ii. Protestants articulated their relationship with God by means of a **covenant theology** articulated by a learned ministry and a devout laity.
   iii. Puritans settled **Massachusetts Bay** with 20,000 souls in what has been called the Great Migration between 1629 and 1639.
   iv. Close ties of extended families, corporate communities, and church life characterized **Puritan family life** in the seventeenth century.
   v. **Conversion, dissent, and expansion** marked the inevitable movement away from the closed corporate communities of the early years of settlement.
   vi. Puritans established forms of self-government through **congregations, towns, and colony governments**.
   vii. Controversy over **infant Baptism and new dissent** caused repeated crises in New England's Congregational churches, the most important of which resulted in the articulation of the **Half-Way Covenant**.

    f. The **English Civil Wars** temporarily halted the progress of North American colonization between 1640 and 1660.

    g. The **first Restoration Colonies** followed closely on the heels of the restoration of Charles II in 1660.

        i. **James Harrington and the Aristocratic Ideal** of a self-governed land of enlightened landholders figured prominently in the foundation of the Carolinas.

        (Show Transparency 02-08: Map, Early Carolina, circa 1710)

       ii. The colony of **New York** proved a failed **experiment in absolutism** but thrived as a diverse colony of traders and landowners.

        (Show Transparency 02-09: Map, The Duke of York's Colonial Charter)

     iii. William Penn founded Pennsylvania as a colony of **Brotherly Love** dominated by the **Quakers,** whose religious and familial beliefs made the colony unique and attractive for immigrants.

        (Show Transparency 02-10: Map, Early Pennsylvania and New Jersey, circa 1700)

American Album: Religious Liberty and Its Perils

Conclusion: It took the nations of northwest Europe some time to plant colonies in the Western Hemisphere, but by 1600 they had begun to expand in earnest. Within a century, the French, Dutch, and English had effectively challenged Spanish domination of the Atlantic frontier and had firmly established colonies throughout the Atlantic coast of North America.

TEACHING RESOURCES

The Magna Carta is an examination of the origins and historical significance of one of the most important documents of Anglo-American political culture. Films for the Humanities (22 minutes).

America: The Newfound Land, narrated by Alistair Cooke, discusses how the British decimated the Indians and out-dueled the Spanish and French for North America. BBC/Time-Life Video (52 minutes).

Colonizing North America: Early Settlements depicts the lives of early settlers, from Jamestown through the turn of the eighteenth century. Filmic Archives (18 minutes).

The Enterprise of England offers an analysis of the reign of Elizabeth I. BBC Video (58 minutes).

America: Home Away from Home examines the Puritan, Pilgrim, and Quaker settlements of the East Coast. Narrated by Alistair Cooke. BBC/Time-Life Video (52 minutes).

Plimoth Plantation reveals the life of Plymouth colony in the year 1627 as told by its "residents." VideoTours History Collection (30 minutes).

Chapter 3

England Discovers Its Colonies: Empire, Liberty, and Expansion

CHAPTER SUMMARY

The seventeenth century witnessed England's simultaneous establishment of far-flung colonies over a thousand miles of British North America and its rise to prominence among its European rivals. Remarkably, these developments occurred during a century of political and social turmoil. By 1700, England could wield great power on both sides of the Atlantic Ocean.

In the aftermath of the Puritan Revolution, Parliament and, later, the restored Stuart monarchy "discovered" England's colonial possessions. The Chesapeake colonies, if not flourishing, had evolved into permanent settlements based largely on tobacco production, while the New England colonies had prospered. By 1660, Massachusetts alone boasted a population of over forty thousand.

Equipped with the principles of mercantilism, the government of Charles II empowered the Lords of Trade to oversee the colonies, as well as to ensure the adequate exploitation of the economic potential of its colonial possessions. The centerpiece of the mercantilist doctrine was the Navigation Acts, a host of strictures designed to make the mother country prosper by regulating trade within the empire. The aim of these Restoration acts was nothing less than to bring order, if not uniformity, to its far-flung colonial possessions.

The Glorious Revolution of 1688 convulsed the empire on both sides of the Atlantic. The fall of the Stuarts ensured that the power of the monarchy, when it was restored in 1692, would be greatly circumscribed. Republican ideals of liberty and checks upon governmental authority took root in the colonies at least as much, if not more, than in England. After a century of upheaval, warfare, and civil strife, England had become the most powerful nation in Europe, while its citizens—both in England and America—enjoyed substantial liberty.

The Indians suffered greatly from the expansion of provincial America. As European settlers joined their American-born peers in pushing farther inland, they brought with them the same problems that had beset the coastal Indian tribes: disease, alcohol, and an insatiable desire for land. When the inevitable crisis came, the French and the Spanish proved rather better than the English in working out reasonable solutions. New France won and held the cooperation of most Indians of the interior who lived east of the Mississippi. Although Indians masterfully played off one European power against another, they retreated increasingly farther inland in order to protect themselves and preserve their way of life.

LIBERTY, EQUALITY, POWER: A THEMATIC BRAID

Perhaps in no century was power more "up for grabs" in England than in the seventeenth. Two revolutions and a regicide attest to that. And while a monarch ruled the empire at both the beginning and the end of the century, by 1700 his ability to wield arbitrary power had diminished greatly, while the effective power of the English state had increased greatly. From Oliver Cromwell to John Locke, the English people had explained their successive overthrows of autocratic rulers by appealing to liberty. While only a few radicals agitated for equality, many English subjects fought earnestly for increased personal liberty under the rule of a less-powerful monarchy. In doing so, they developed the basic tenets of republicanism, including constitutionalism, mixed government, and the right of legitimate opposition.

The wild gyrations of revolution and restoration convulsed England's colonies. Every colony witnessed some form of rebellion or unrest, from Bacon's Rebellion in Virginia and Leisler's Rebellion in New York to the Salem witch trials in Massachusetts. By the end of the century, the colonies and the mother country converged toward representative government in the hope of defending liberty against the encroachment of corrupt central authority. Ultimately, liberty flourished even more in the colonies than it did in the mother country, though more in some colonies than in others.

IDENTIFICATIONS

Mercantilism	Navigation Acts
enumerated commodities	Lords of Trade
King Philip's (Metacom's) War	Iroquois Nations
Onontia	Middle Ground
James II	Dominion of New England
William Berkeley	Bacon's Rebellion
Glorious Revolution	Jacob Leisler
Salem witch trials	William III
Imperial federalism	mixed and balanced Constitution
Edmund Andros	King William's War
Sir Robert Walpole	Queen Anne's War
Louisiana	la Salle
Popé	Taos Pueblo Revolt

CHRONOLOGY

1651	First of the Navigation Acts.
1675	Metacom's (King Philip's) War begins in New England.
	Lords of Trade created.
1673	Jacques Marquette and Louis Joliet explore the Mississippi.
1676	Bacon's Rebellion in Virginia.
1680	Pueblo Indian Revolt.
1683	New York Charter of Liberties.
1685	James II becomes king of England.
	Louis XIV revokes Edict of Nantes.
1686–1689	Dominion of New England.
1688	Glorious Revolution in England.

1689	Leisler's Rebellion in New York.
	William and Mary ascend to English throne.
	Andros is overthrown in Boston.
	Catholic government is overthrown in Maryland.
1689–1697	King William's War.
1692	Salem witch trials.
1696	Creation of the Board of Trade.
1699	First permanent French settlement in Louisiana.
1702–1713	War of Spanish Succession (Queen Anne's War).
1707	Act of Union joins England and Scotland.
1721–1742	Robert Walpole ministry.

THEMATIC TOPICS FOR ENRICHMENT

1. What were the differences between Whigs and Tories in seventeenth-century England? What contributions did each faction make to the creation of British political culture?

2. How did the Glorious Revolution in England destroy absolutism and guarantee representative government in British North America?

3. In what ways did the Spanish, French, and English empires develop differently from one another?

4. Discuss the ways in which Indian tribes took advantage of—and, in turn, were taken advantage of by—the imperial conflicts among Spain, France, and England.

5. What factors led to a remarkable increase in the population of the British colonies of North America after 1660?

6. In what ways were colonial households similar to their English counterparts, and in what ways were they different?

7. Explain the consequences for both Indians and European settlers of the numerous Indian wars between 1690 and 1716.

GEOGRAPHY OBJECTIVES

1. On a map of Virginia, trace the geographic features of Bacon's Rebellion (p. 103).

2. Identify which British colonies in North America at the beginning of the eighteenth century were royal, proprietary, or corporate (p. 111).

3. Draw the outlines of the North American possessions of Spain and France in the early eighteenth century (p. 117).

4. On a map of North America, fill in the names of the British colonies along the eastern seaboard (p. 111).

SUGGESTED ESSAY TOPICS

1. Discuss the relationship between England's commerce and its colonies.

2. Evaluate the various Indian strategies of survival in North America in the years after European colonization.

3. Define the term *mercantilism* and explain its significance for British colonial policy. In what ways did the Navigation Acts express mercantilistic ideas?

4. What do you think the authors mean by the metaphor "spectrum of settlement" to describe England's colonial possessions (3-2)?

5. Discuss the development of the colonies in terms of demography, race, religion, and economy.

LECTURE OUTLINE

1. In many ways the Atlantic Ocean functioned as a prism refracting English aims into **the spectrum of settlement** of North America.

    (Show Transparency 03-02: Map, Area of English Settlement by 1700)

    a. The colonies featured profound Demographic Differences from one region to the next with New England's salubrious climate at one extreme and the sugar islands of the Caribbean at the other.

    b. The English colonies also featured profound differences from one another in **race, ethnicity, and economy**; the colonies comprised four distinct regions: New England, the Middle Colonies, the Chesapeake, and the Deep South.

    c. Although most colonists were Protestant, **religious** differences within colonies and among them stood out as one of North America's unique social features.

    d. **Local and provincial government** also varied throughout the colonies, from proprietorships to royal colonies; some colonies boasted rather open, democratic governments, while others proved more autocratic.

    e. The colonies did boast some **unifying trends**, including those of **language, war** (common enemies), **law, and inheritance**.

2. The **beginnings of empire** stemmed from England's growing realization that the colonies served vital needs both economically and politically.

    a. The **critical 1640s** were a time of **upheaval in America**, characterized by Indian warfare, instability, and a general lack of direction from England.

    b. The most important imperial innovation proved to be the advent of the **mercantilist** system, which historians have called part of a **moral revolution**.

        i. Following the Thirty Years' War, Parliament passed the **First Navigation Act** banning foreign ships in the colonies.

        ii. The **Restoration Navigation Acts** were a crucial series of measures that sought to oversee virtually all aspects of colonial trade, "enumerating" commodities, as well as regulating goods going to and from England's outposts.

3. Growing conflicts between **Indians and settlers** led to a number of conflagrations as both parties sought to master their new relationships.

    a. **Indian strategies of survival** varied greatly, from outright warfare to conversion and alliance.

    b. Among the most promising, if ultimately unsuccessful, attempts to attain a modus vivendi between settlers and the local inhabitants were the **Puritan Indian missions**, which sought to bring Indians into the fold of European civilization and thereby end the strife between the two peoples.

    c. Cultural differences and colonists' insatiable appetite for land led to **Metacom's (or King Philip's) War** in 1675, a bloody conflagration in which some 800 settlers and an unknown number of Indians perished.

    (Show Transparency 03-03: Map: New England in Metacom's War, 1675–1676)

    d. **Virginia's Indian War** during the governorship of Sir William Berkeley caused great insecurity on the frontier for several years.

    e. Led by the recent immigrant Nathaniel Bacon, **Bacon's Rebellion** of 1675–1676 resulted in the devastation of much of Virginia and the temporary collapse of royal government.

    (Show Transparency 03-04: Map, Bacon's Rebellion in Virginia, 1676)

4. Bacon's Rebellion helped to trigger a **crisis in England and the redefinition of empire** in hopes of improving imperial oversight and control.

    a. **The Popish Plot, the Exclusion crisis, and the rise of party** combined to undermine the Stuart monarchy and bring about the Glorious Revolution of 1688.

    b. Indian wars and domestic considerations compelled the Crown to create the **Lords of Trade** and undertake wholesale **imperial reform** in the latter half of the seventeenth century.

    c. In 1685, James II disallowed the New York Charter of Liberties of 1683 and forced New York to join with its northern neighbors to form the **Dominion of New England**.

    d. In overthrowing the Stuart monarchy, the **Glorious Revolution** of 1688 had significant consequences for colonial affairs, leading to what historians call the **Glorious Revolution in America**.

    (Show Transparency 03-05: Map, Government and Religion in the British Colonies, 1720)

      i. Virtually every colony underwent some form of **political crisis in 1688–1689**, including New York, North Carolina, and Maryland.

      ii. At the time when Massachusetts had virtually no central government, the **Salem witch trials** convulsed eastern Massachusetts, resulting in the capital punishment of twenty accused persons.

      iii. The **English response** to the Glorious Revolution in America proved remarkably lenient and sympathetic for the most part, as William and Mary sought reconciliation, not conflict.

    e. The Glorious Revolution dispatched absolutism in the colonies and helped to guarantee that the Completion of Empire would put **representative government** in the colonies on far more sure footing.

      i. **Imperial federalism** is the term used to describe the division of power between the center and the periphery in the empire.

      ii. English people on both sides of the Atlantic viewed with pride their unwritten **mixed and balanced Constitution**, which included institutional authority along the Aristotelian model of one, few, and many.

5. The tenuous coexistence of the **contrasting empires** of England, France, and Spain erupted into war after the Glorious Revolution.

a. In 1680, a San Juan Pueblo medicine man led a revolt against the Spaniards know as the **Taos Pueblo Revolt**.

b. Relying more on intelligence than force, **New France** maintained a strong colonial presence in the Saint Lawrence and Mississippi valleys in a region called the **Middle Ground**.

(Show Transparency 03-06: Map, French Middle Ground, circa 1700)

c. France and Spain were considerably less successful at maintaining peace in their imperial possessions in **French Louisiana and Spanish Texas**.

6. With a population of at least 250,000 settlers by 1700 and an explosive growth rate, the **British colonies** could fairly be called **an empire of settlement**.

a. The key institution of the engine of British expansion proved to be the **colonial household**, the center of economic production and reproduction.

b. Householders carried their quest for independence outside the home, embracing a **voluntaristic ethic** as the personal codes of both private life and **public life**.

c. France, Spain, and England devolved into **three warring empires** from **1689** through **1716**.

(Show Transparency 03-07: Map, Northeastern Theater of War, 1689–1713; and Transparency 03-08: Map, Southeastern Theater of War 1702–1713)

American Album: Religious Strife, Liberty, and the Clash of Empires

Conclusion: In the course of the seventeenth century, England became a global giant in large measure on the basis of its American colonies and the important economic role they played in the empire. Fitting perfectly into the mercantilist scheme, colonies served as markets for finished goods and supplied vital raw materials to the mother country.

TEACHING RESOURCES

Where America Began explores the life and culture of seventeenth-century Jamestown. VideoTours History Collection (60 minutes).

Colonial America recalls America's earliest days, when empires were competing for the continent. Mastervision Humanities Series (52 minutes).

Black Robe is a stunning portrait of the challenges facing Jesuit missionaries. Vidmark Films (80 minutes).

Unearthing the Slave Trade shows how archaeologists attempt to reconstruct the lives of African Americans in the colonies. Films for the Humanities (60 minutes).

Indians Among Us describes the upheaval resulting from the clash of cultures between Indians and European settlers. Re-Discovering America (60 minutes).

Chapter 4
Provincial America and the Struggle for a Continent

CHAPTER SUMMARY

After 1715, the European colonies in provincial America underwent a transformation from settlement to society. While the colonies of Spain, France, and England developed in quite different ways, each experienced similar strains. Indian problems, intercolonial warfare, and the great difficulties entailed in moving into the interior of the continent played havoc with even the most far-sighted imperial schemes.

Through the first half of the eighteenth century, the three empires in North America fought one another. While the main theater of strife continued to be Europe, the possession of North America became increasingly important. Control of North America promised valuable raw materials, ample space for colonization, and increased control over the Indians. Yet, with so much at stake, neither the Spanish, the French, nor the English had the ability to extinguish the others. Well into the eighteenth century, the English control of North America proved elusive.

Indian problems and imperial strife failed to slow the acceleration of immigrants into the colonies. Joined by increasing numbers of Scots and Irish, the English continued to seek a better life in North America. For many, expansion and Anglicization promised greater liberty and an improving standard of living. The British colonies, but not the French or Spanish, also began to participate in the European Enlightenment, partly because they established their own newspapers. In the 1730s and 1740s, they experienced a massive religious revival—the Great Awakening—the first of its kind in world history.

With the great influx of settlers, England's North American possessions developed characteristics more like those of the mother country. This process of Anglicization had a profound impact on all aspects of colonial society. Declining dangers of the frontier and a more stable economy benefited many, while simultaneouly exacerbating problems for women, slaves, and the poorest of society. Anglicization ultimately led to political conflict with England.

By the middle of the eighteenth century, the British empire had achieved imperial domination in North America. After marginal victories in King William's War, Queen Anne's War, and King George's War, Britain and its North American colonies roundly defeated the French in the Seven Years' War, partly because Spain remained neutral for most of that war. In no small measure, then, the year 1763 marked the high point of the empire in both England and North America. It is all the more remarkable that relations between the firmly secure colonies and the mother country should have deteriorated so rapidly after 1763.

While always proclaiming allegiance to king and country, the colonists nevertheless fiercely defended their political rights. Considering themselves equal citizens within the empire, colonists vigorously protected their indigenous political institutions. As in England, colonial politics provided a venue primarily for the well connected. Farmers, laborers, transients, and backcountry folk found themselves on the periphery of the political structure. In the course of the eighteenth century, colonial politics featured a "country" and "court" division similar to that in England. Most disputes erupted between governors and their councils on the one hand, and the colonial assemblies on the other. The former vigorously enforced imperial prerogative, upon which their authority depended, while the latter defended colonial rights and privileges. Through the French and Indian War, colonial governors and assemblies resolved most conflicts amicably, for they needed each other to make the colonies function. As often as not, governors and imperial placemen let the colonies go with a minimum of imperial imposition. In return, placemen made their fortunes and went their way.

The French and Indian War, or the Seven Years' War, abruptly intensified imperial interest in the colonies. While the wars of King William and Queen Anne had spilled over into North America, the French and Indian conflict centered in the colonies. As a result, imperial authority, in the form of redcoats, the navy, placemen, and the like, grew steadily in what turned out to be a long and bloody fight. The course of the war and the changes in imperial policy combined to create conflict between officials sworn to prosecute the war most vigorously and colonists who had grown accustomed to officials that seldom sought to enforce many otherwise onerous rules and regulations.

The colonists played their part as members of the empire during the imperial conflicts of the eighteenth century. They well understood that their liberty and freedom, which they so greatly prized, depended on their membership in the British empire. British power ensured colonial liberty.

Liberty, Equality, Power: A Thematic Braid

The expansion and Anglicization of provincial America meant greater liberty and greater power for its inhabitants. By the middle of the eighteenth century, victories over their French and Spanish rivals afforded colonists a great deal of opportunity and freedom. British power fostered colonial liberty.

Expansion and diversification did not result in equality. Far from it. While many colonists enjoyed increased wealth and privileges, they often did so at the expense of others. Some losers were opponents of the empire, such as the French, the Spanish, and their Indian allies, while other losers were part of the empire. Expansion into the interior of North America provided opportunity to many, but at significant cost. Indian wars, disease, and brutal living conditions plagued the backcountry. And, in every colony, slavery had become an important, often vital, source of labor. Yet, as the availability of slaves increased, colonists' wealth and status became tied to the exploitation of others. By the middle of the eighteenth century, slavery had become a key support of English liberty, particularly in the southern colonies. Power and liberty had their costs.

Virtually all subjects of the empire agreed that Britain's astonishing rise to great–power status was the result of a unique system of mixed and balanced constitutional government. Imperial victories proved a sign of beneficent government. In sum, British power was essentially intertwined with British liberty.

Similarly, British subjects on both sides of the Atlantic well understood the importance of British imperial vigilance for the maintenance of liberty. The French in Canada and the Spanish in Florida made it particularly clear to colonists that their liberty had a cost. When called upon to make sacrifices for the defense of the empire, the colonists for the most part responded with material and manpower, even when they were not directly threatened. Although they failed to agree to Franklin's Albany Plan, the colonists fought vigorously in the French and Indian War. In the course of nine years of warfare, many colonies played important roles in the final victory. They believed they had defended their liberty with skill and bravery.

Identifications

gang labor	task system
Charleston	Eliza Lucas Pinckney
staple crop	cash bounty

Hanoverian Dynasty	Gullah
redemptioners	paper money
Georgia	John Peter Zenger
Cato's Letters	Enlightenment
Benjamin Franklin	Guy Fawkes' Day
James Oglethorpe	Scots-Irish
Great Awakening	George Whitefield
Gilbert Tennent	Jonathan Edwards
Old Side/New Side	Baptists
Methodism	John Tillotson
Zabdiel Boylston	Shepherd's Tent
John Witherspoon	King's College
de Mosé	Alexander Spotswood
William Shirley	Fort Louisbourg
Fort Oswego	Stono Uprising
wampum	Louisiana
War of Jenkins' Ear	Fort Duquesne
Treaty of Aix-la-Chapelle	Acadian expulsion
Albany Congress	Ohio Company of Virginia
French and Indian War	General Edward Braddock
Great Meadows	William Pitt
Fort William Massacre	Montcalm and Wolfe
Cherokee War	Peace of Paris

CHRONOLOGY

1704	*Boston News-letter* becomes first newspaper in British colonies.
1714	George I brings the Hanoverian dynasty to the British throne.
1715–1716	Yamassee War in South Carolina.
1722	New Orleans founded.
1727	George II suceeds George I.
1730s–1740s	Great Awakening.
1732–1733	Founding of Georgia.
1733	Molasses Act.
1735	Zenger Trial.
1739	George Whitefield's second trip to British colonies.
	Stono Rebellion.
1739–1742	War of Jenkins' Ear.
1741	New York slave conspiracy trials.
1744–1748	King George's War.
1748	Treaty of Aix-la-Chapelle.
1754	Washington surrenders at Great Meadows.
	Albany Congress.
1755	Edward Braddock defeated.

	Acadians expelled.
1756–1763	Seven Years' War (French and Indian War).
1757	William Pitt becomes war minister.
1759	Wolfe defeats Montcalm on Plains of Abraham.
1760	Accession of George III as king of Great Britain.
	Cherokee War devastates Carolina backcountry.
1763	Peace of Paris.

THEMATIC TOPICS FOR ENRICHMENT

1. How did the massive influx of African slaves between 1700 and 1740 transform the social structure of the southern colonies?

2. What was "householder autonomy" and what factors threatened to undermine it?

3. How did life in the backcountry differ from that on the coast?

4. Discuss the changing role of women throughout the eighteenth century.

5. Why was the utopian experiment in Georgia such a failure?

6. What were the unique features of South Carolina? Contrast gang labor with the task system.

7. Why were the Mid-Atlantic colonies considered to be the "best poor man's country"?

8. What were the key features of denomination reallignment in the Great Awakening?

9. List the colonial colleges of the eighteenth century and the dates they were founded.

10. Compare the power of the colonial governors with that of the colonial assemblies.

11. Detail the main features of British opposition ideology.

12. Assess the military aspects of the French and Indian War. In what ways did the conflict lead to misunderstandings between colonists and the mother country?

GEOGRAPHY OBJECTIVES

1. Distinguish the colonies of the Upper South with those of the Lower South (p. 162).

2. Find the Georgia colony on a map. It was meant to be a buffer between which two areas (p. 151)?

3. Locate the main regions where Indian tribes could play off one colonial power against another (p. 154).

4. Find Fort Duquesne, Fort Oswego, and Lake George on a map of North America in the years of the French and Indian War (p. 154).

5. Sketch out the British conquest of Canada from 1758 through 1760. Identify which American colonies were closest to the conflict (p. 161).

SUGGESTED ESSAY TOPICS

1. Discuss the process of Anglicization in the colonies to 1750. How did the colonists seek "to emulate their homeland?" (4-1)?

2. What was the role of religion in the settlement and growth of the North American colonies?

3. Define the term *Enlightenment*. In what ways did colonial development reflect Enlightenment ideas?

4. Detail the basic features of government in the American colonies. What were the major similarities and differences between the government of the mother country and that of the colonies?

LECTURE OUTLINE

1. Competing social and economic pressures compelled colonists to attempt to reconcile provincial desire for uncontrolled expansion with England's attempts toward **Anglicization.**

   (Show Transparency 04-01: British Ad (1738) Encouraging Scots-Irish to Move to New York)

   a. Economic inequality in a number of circumstances led directly to a **threat to householder autonomy**, as the economy of colonial America became more complex and differentiated.
   b. Changes from settlement to a stratified society led colonists toward **anglicizing the role of women**, a change that had both advantages and disadvantages for women.

2. The eighteenth century witnessed dramatic changes in North America as territorial expansion and growing numbers of immigrants brought about **regional differentiation** within the empire.
   a. Immigration and the advent of plantation slavery on a large scale signaled the emergence of the **Old South**, characterized by the production of staple crops for export.
   b. With the phenomenal growth of Pennsylvania and New Jersey, the Mid-Atlantic colonies came to be known as the **"best poor man's country."**
   c. The growth and social differentiation of the coast ensured that the **backcountry** would be a distinct region, sparsely settled, relatively dangerous, and politically underrepresented.
   d. In the course of the eighteenth century, New England suffered from a faltering economy and currency problems related in part to the circulation of **paper money**.

3. What made these diverse regions more alike was their slow process of **Anglicization**, or the slow development of more English characteristics.
   a. Although few colonists owned books or engaged in intellectual debate the **world of print** was spreading its way through the colonies.
   b. The **Enlightenment in America**, in both its religious and secular forms, transformed colonists' assumptions and modes of thinking.
   c. As in England, **lawyers and doctors** began to emerge as part of a coterie of professionals with growing prestige and power.
   d. Founded in 1732–1733, **Georgia** failed as Enlightenment Utopia imagined by its founders; it became just another southern colony dominated by slavery and local exigencies.

4. The **Great Awakening** convulsed religious institutions and virtually all of society in provincial America.

a. The **origins of the revivals** remain obscure but may be tied to the rise of a new generation of ministers with decidedly novel ideas.

b. Many historians date the beginning of religious enthusiasm in America to **George Whitefield** launching the transatlantic revivals, particularly in his second trip to the colonies in 1739.

c. The revivals caused **disruptions** in virtually every colony that took years to die down.

d. Historians have debated the exact **long-term consequences of the revivals**, but they agree that the Great Awakening affected almost every colonial community.

    i. Religious schisms from the revivals resulted in the establishment of a number of **new colleges**.

    ii. The **denominational realignment** that ensued from the awakenings is a unique feature of American religion.

5. A mixture of local and English traditions, the **political culture in the colonies** developed rapidly in the eighteenth century.

a. The two key institutional developments were the **rise of the assembly** and the governor's growing responsibilities.

b. The southern colonies had **"Country Constitutions,"** that emphasized the importance of restricting corruption and central power.

c. **"Court Constitutions"** were characteristic of the northern colonies, where powerful councils closely advised imperial governors.

6. Contention with France and Spain led to a **renewal of imperial conflict** by midcentury.

a. The colonists were eager to offer **challenges to French power** in the interior regions of North America.

(Show Transparency 04-02: Map, French Louisiana and Spanish Texas, circa 1730)

b. The danger of **slave revolts and war with Spain** grew in the first decades of the century, ultimately culminating in the Stono Rebellion and the War of Jenkins' Ear in 1739.

(Show Transparency 04-03: Map, Caribbean Theater of War, 1739–1742)

c. In 1744, France joined Spain to fight Britain in **King George's War**, in which untrained Yankee volunteers subdued the great French fortress of Louisbourg on June 16, 1745.

(Show Transparency 04-04: Map, Southeastern Theater of War, 1739–1742)

d. All of these conflicts merely foreshadowed **the impending storm** that would take place after midcentury.

7. The **war for North America** occurred between 1755 and 1763.

(Show Transparency 04-05: Map, France Versus Britain in North America by 1755)

a. Ben Franklin's 1754 plan for the **Albany Congress** to discuss mutual defense proved an utter failure at the onset of war.

(Show Transparency 04-06: Map, British Offensives, 1755)

b. The first years of the French and Indian War, especially with the death of **General Edward Braddock**, proved to be bitter years filled with British defeats.

c. Years of war and uncertainty led to grave imperial tensions as successive administrations from **Loudoun to Pitt** failed to satisfy the Crown.

   (Show Transparency 04-07: Map, Conquest of Canada, 1758–1760)

d. The years 1760–1763 can be termed the **years of British victory**, as the war finally became clearly winnable.

   (Show Transparency 04-08: Map, Growth of Population to 1760)

e. In an effort to take advantage of the great burden of England's war with France, southern Indians commenced the **Cherokee War**, while the Spanish intervened in the South.

f. The **Peace of Paris** of 1763 marked the pinnacle of the first British Empire.

American Album: The Refined and the Crude

Conclusion: As the colonists of provincial America struggled to secure more land and greater security, they created a socially stratified society of richer and poorer, ins and outs, that increasingly resembled England through the eighteenth century. The costs and consequences of a succession of imperial struggles set the stage for the demise of the empire.

TEACHING RESOURCES

Multicultural Peoples of North America video series. This collection celebrates the varied cultural heritage of different cultural groups. Includes videos on African Americans and the Amish. Filmic Archives (30 minutes each).

Working for the Lord depicts American religious development into the nineteenth century. Republic Pictures Home Video (52 minutes).

The Inventory examines the life of a typical middle-class family in the eighteenth century through an examination of its possessions and values. Films for the Humanities (28 minutes).

Old Salem and *Cavaliers and Craftsmen—Williamsburg* depict life in two of America's oldest communities through both a social and historical approach. VideoTours History Collection (30 minutes each).

Colonial America: Life in the Maturing Colonies focuses on the colonies between the turn of the eighteenth century and the French and Indian War. Filmic Archives (17 minutes).

From Waalstraat to Wall Street explores the development of English New York from its Dutch roots as New Amsterdam. Films for the Humanities (50 minutes).

The Battle of Quebec: 1759, The End of the French and Indian War describes the Battle of Quebec while analyzing the causes of the French and Indian War from a Canadian perspective. Films for the Humanities (32 minutes).

In Search of the Dream: Unearthing the Slave Trade examines slavery in New York City through a close review of the archaeological records unearthed in lower Manhattan. Films for the Humanities (28 minutes).

The Last of the Mohicans is a feature film starring Daniel Day Lewis that gives a strong dramatization of the James Fenimore Cooper tale about the French and Indian War.

Chapter 5
Reform, Resistance, Revolution

CHAPTER SUMMARY

England's costly victory in the French and Indian War demonstrated the strategic importance of North America in the British empire. After the signing of the Peace of Paris in 1763, the new Grenville administration wasted little time in implementing a series of measures that demonstrated Britain's commitment to keeping the colonies under greater supervision. The Proclamation Line; the Sugar, Currency, and Quartering Acts; and the fateful Stamp Act put the imperial government on a collision course with the colonies. Colonists of all stripes, from New Hampshire to Georgia, came together as never before in protest against what they perceived to be a great and impossible usurpation of their British rights and liberties.

Through a series of three successive crises, the relationship between Britain and its North American colonies deteriorated to the brink of revolution. When the thirteen colonies declared their independence in 1776, it was not what either side had expected or desired just a decade earlier.

The first imperial crisis stemmed from the Stamp Act of 1765. When Parliament passed the act over the vocal objections of colonists like Benjamin Franklin and a number of members of Parliament, it considered its actions in line with previous imperial measures. The colonists felt differently, believing that the Stamp Act was an attempt to raise revenue, not to regulate trade. As such, it was an unconstitutional attempt by Parliament to confiscate colonists' property; taxation was something only the colonial assemblies could undertake. Through coordinated action and the vigilante activism of the "Sons of Liberty," the colonies (save Georgia) managed to keep stamped paper from ever being circulated. Although Parliament issued a ringing Declaratory Act, it repealed the loathsome and unenforceable Stamp Act. The colonists jubilantly celebrated their victory.

Smarting from the Stamp Act rebuke, many members of Parliament eagerly welcomed Charles Townshend's claim that he had devised a means to impose taxes on the recalcitrant colonists. Townshend argued that the colonies would agree to duties on tea, lead, glass, and other enumerated imports. He would simply couch the duties in terms of the long-standing Navigation Acts. Townshend could not have been more in error. Summarily rejecting his distinction between internal and external taxation, the colonists again organized resistance to parliamentary actions. In this case, they formulated a nonimportation agreement in which colonial merchants would not import British goods. Once again, Parliament eventually backed down, averting a prolonged crisis by repealing all of the Townshend duties except the one on tea.

The third and final crisis stemmed from another fateful act of Parliament, this one designed to induce the colonists to buy duties tea. In response, Boston's Sons of Liberty threw several shiploads of East India Tea Company tea into Boston Harbor. The ensuing severe reaction of Parliament, known as the Coercive Acts, precipitated concerted colonial action, especially the First and Second Continental Congresses, which took the first steps toward independence. By April of 1775, the colonists and the British empire were at war. Independence came fifteen months later.

The same misunderstandings, fears, and lack of mutual trust that had led to the imperial crises and the Boston Massacre proved too deep-seated to repair by negotiation. Neither the Olive Branch Petition nor any other attempts at reconciliation could stem the growing movement toward American independence. By July 4, 1776, the colonies had rejected all parliamentary authority and, with the help of Thomas Paine's radical *Common Sense*, severed their ties to the British monarchy. When the Continental Congress adopted the Declaration of Independence, the United States came into being.

LIBERTY, EQUALITY, POWER: A THEMATIC BRAID

Inevitably, when king and Parliament began a course of imperial reforms in the immediate aftermath of the French and Indian War, the colonists responded with dismay. Convinced they had paid their fair share in defense of their liberty, many colonists argued that their liberty was now under siege on a new front. This new enemy, if left unchecked, would likewise destroy colonial liberty. Once again, colonists had to defend liberty against overgreat power.

In 1776, when Thomas Jefferson declared "all men are created equal," he surely did not mean everyone in colonial America. The colonies on the eve of independence were home to several hundred thousand slaves without the prospect of freedom, as well as a million white women who were legally dependent on men. Jefferson seems to have had in mind a more circumscribed proposition—that colonists and Englishmen ought to enjoy identical political rights. Since king and Parliament proved unwilling to acknowledge colonial rights, the American colonies had to create their own nation.

For the colonies, the movement toward independence was an attempt to protect liberty more than to further it. By 1776, the British empire, long the protector of colonial liberty, had come to threaten its destruction. The colonies had to take action.

By 1775, only the British army and navy were holding the empire together. Confident of their growing power, which was reflected in their collective responses to the three successive imperial crises, the American colonies felt compelled to defend their liberty against imperial aggression. The revolutionaries formed the Continental Congress, created a national army, and prepared for a bitter struggle to protect liberty and demonstrate their equality. They had not yet faced the problem of whether they could protect their liberties without creating a strong central government of their own.

IDENTIFICATIONS

George III
John Wilkes
Paxton Boys
Sugar Act
Quartering Act
Sons of Liberty
Ebenezer McIntosh
Stamp Act Congress
Patrick Henry
William Pitt

Grenville Administration
Proclamation of 1763
Pontiac's War
Currency Act
Stamp Act
Daniel Dulany
virtual representation
nonimportation agreements
Massachusetts Circular Letter

Letters of a Pennsylvania Farmer   regulator movement
Battle of Alamance Creek   Castle William
feudal revival   Boston Massacre
Gaspée affair   Tea Act
Sarah Osborn   Declaratory Act
Phillis Wheatley   Revenue Act of 1766
Thomas Hutchinson   Townshend Revenue Act
Thomas Gage   Coercive Acts (Intolerable Acts)
Quebec Act   Paxton Boys
Continental Congress   Battle of Bunker (Breed's) Hill
Olive Branch Petition   Battle of Lexington and Concord
Thomas Paine   Committee of Public Safety
Declaration of Independence   *Common Sense*
Paul Revere   Lord Dunmore

CHRONOLOGY

1763	Peace of Paris.
	George Grenville administration begins.
	Pontiac's War.
	Proclamation of 1763.
1764	Sugar and Currency Acts passed by Parliament.
1765	Stamp and Quartering Acts passed.
	Rockingham replaces Grenville.
1765–1766	First Imperial Crisis.
1766	Pitt replaces Rockingham.
	Revenue Act passed.
1767	Townshend Duties passed by Parliament.
	Grafton replaces Pitt.
	John Dickinson publishes *Letters*.
1767–1770	Second Imperial Crisis.
1768	John Hancock's sloop *Liberty* seized.
1770	Boston Massacre.
1771	Regulators defeated at Alamance Creek, North Carolina.
1772	British customs vessel *Gaspée* burned.
	Colonies create committees of correspondence.
1773	Tea Act passed by Parliament.
	Boston Tea Party.
1773–1776	Third Imperial Crisis.
1774	Quebec Act.
	Coercive Acts imposed.
	First Continental Congress.
1775	Battles of Lexington and Concord.

Second Continental Congress.

Battle of Bunker Hill.

Lord Dunmore's Proclamation.

Olive Branch Petition sent to King George III.

1776   Thomas Paine publishes *Common Sense*.

Battle of Dorchester Heights.

Battle of Moore's Creek Bridge.

Declaration of Independence.

THEMATIC TOPICS FOR ENRICHMENT

1. What was "virtual representation"? Explain why the colonies so vigorously rejected the idea. Why did they similarly decline actual representation in Parliament?

2. Why did Parliament repeal the Stamp Act? What was the point of repealing the Stamp Act, yet passing the Declaratory Act?

3. Was the colonial distinction between regulation and taxation a legitimate one? Was there any precedent for such a distinction in English history?

4. What was the "feudal revival"? Assess its significance for Revolutionary America.

5. Discuss the meaning of liberty to women and slaves. How was it distinct from the liberty of white males?

6. How did the government of George III change its tactics for punishing the colonies after the Boston Massacre, the *Gaspée* affair, and the Boston Tea Party? By the third imperial crisis, was the empire held together solely by force?

GEOGRAPHY OBJECTIVES

1. Trace the extent of the Proclamation Line of 1763 (p. 170).

2. Locate the colonies in which the great estates of the feudal revival covered the largest extent of land (p. 187).

3. Find Lexington and Concord in relation to the city of Boston (p. 197).

SUGGESTED ESSAY TOPICS

1. The historian Lawrence Henry Gipson once argued that, if there had been no French and Indian War, the American Revolution would not have occurred, at least not when it did. Make a case both for and against Gipson's claim.

2. Some historians have claimed that the era of the American Revolution was characterized by paranoia. Does this description make sense? What underlying fears drove Britain into its imperial reforms? What aspects of these reforms made the colonies fear for their liberties? Were these fears justified on either side? On both sides?

3. How did thirteen disparate colonies that had failed all attempts at collective actions before 1763 manage to unite and declare their independence by 1776?

LECTURE OUTLINE

1. King and Parliament began a large-scale process of **imperial reform** in response to waging a costly war in North America.
   a. The **Bute ministry,** led by the King's principal advisor, John Stuart, began the first steps toward reducing Britain's foreign financial obligations.
   b. After the arrest of John Wilkes, the **Grenville ministry** inaugurated an ambitious program intended to effect better administration of the colonies, augmenting revenues in particular.
      i. Tailored to meet treaty obligations, Grenville's Indian policy rested on the **Proclamation line of 1763,** which sought to restrict colonists' encroachment onto Indian lands.
      ii. **Pontiac's War** of 1763 caught many frontier folk by surprise, but the Ottawa chief's (and the other tribes') aggression failed to halt—or even slow down—European penetration into the interior of the continent.

      (Show Transparency 05-02: Map, Pontiac's War and the Proclamation Line of 1763)

   c. The **Sugar Act** sought to increase revenue and inhibit smuggling by simultaneously lowering duties on molasses and making it more profitable for customs officers to prosecute violators of the Navigation Acts.
   d. Following closely on the heels of the Sugar Act, the **Currency Act and the Quartering Act** respectively constituted bold new regulation of colonial "paper" currency and restated the colonists' obligations to quarter his majesty's troops.
   e. The **Stamp Act** sought to raise revenue in the colonies by means of a tax on all official documents.

2. Colonial dismay at the Stamp Act and the other parliamentary initiatives since 1763 climaxed in the **Stamp Act Crisis**, as colonists gathered in a Stamp Act Congress to fight Parliament.
   a. By means of the nonimportation agreement of the Stamp Act Congress and the extralegal initiatives of the **Sons of Liberty,** the colonies sought nullification of the Stamp Act.
   b. Colonial vigilance and pressure from London's suffering merchant community forced Parliament to repeal the dreaded stamp tax, while simultaneously passing the **Declaratory Act.**

3. Relative quiet returned to imperial relations until the eruption of the **Townshend crisis** in 1767.
   a. Named for the chancellor of the exchequer, the **Townshend program** was an ill-fated attempt to raise revenue through "external" taxation on colonial imports such as lead, china, and tea.
   b. Parliament's 1768 experiment in **military coercion** accomplished little more than to convince many colonists that the British government was openly seeking to undermine their liberty.
   c. As colonials saw parallels between their situation and that of John Wilkes, the **second Wilkes crisis** in England reinforced colonial convictions that the King and Parliament were corrupt and power hungry.

d. The **Boston Massacre** of March 5, 1770, marked the failure of Britain's first attempts at military coercion and served to galvanize anti-imperial sentiment throughout North America.

(Show Transparency 05-01: Paul Revere's Engraving of the Bloody Massacre)

e. Rather than bringing about renewed affection, disaffection set in between colonies and mother country despite the **repeal of the Townshend taxes**.

4. After the second imperial crisis, the **contagion of liberty** grew slowly, as colonists faced many internal cleavages.
   a. Although the colonies were moving away from British political domination, many regions witnessed what historians call a **feudal revival**, especially in New York's Hudson Valley, as well as in Maryland and Pennsylvania.
   b. The **regulator movements in the Carolinas** resulted from the remarkable under-representation of rural folk in the low-country dominated houses of assembly.
   c. From the death of **Crispus Attucks** in the Boston Massacre to wives offering their willing support to nonimportation, **slaves and women** responded in a number of meaningful ways to colonial discussions of freedom and liberty.

5. The **last imperial crisis** broke the relative calm of the period 1770–1773, as colonists and mother country failed to resolve amicably their simmering differences.
   a. The **tea crisis** resulted from the Boston Tea party of December 16, 1773, when angry Bostonians threw India Tea Company tea into Boston Harbor.
   b. Britain's response to the Tea Party was a set of **Coercive Acts**, which shut down Boston's port with the intent to force colonial submission.
   c. Instead of restoring order, the Intolerable Acts, as the colonists styled them, resulted in a **radical explosion**, which cowed those who had cautioned against rash actions against England.
   d. The **First Continental Congress** met in Philadelphia in September 1774 to act as the voice of the united colonies.
   e. England's intransigence and colonial unity precipitated the Battles of Lexington and Concord, which inevitably moved the empire **toward war**.

(Show Transparency 05-03: Map, Lexington, Concord, and Boston 1775–1776)

6. The **improvised war** of colonies and mother country, centering primarily in Massachusetts, lasted until the declaration of American independence in the summer of 1776.
   a. The **Second Continental Congress**, which met in Philadelphia from May 1775, organized national defense and acted as the executive for the fledgling United States.
   b. Independence came with the signing of the Declaration of Independence in July 1776.

American Album: American Artists and the Revolution in Painting

Conclusion: In the aftermath of the Peace of Paris, three successive imperial crises convinced England that the colonies desired nothing short of independence, and the colonists that king and Parliament sought to destroy their liberties through an overarching imperial power. The result of this almost paranoid view was the disintegration of the empire.

TEACHING RESOURCES

Liberty: The American Revolution, volumes I–III, tells the story of the coming of the American War for Independence by means of actors reading contemporary writings. PBS Video (60 minutes each).

Private Yankee Doodle views the life and suffering of the average American soldier in the Revolutionary War through the re-creation of a Continental Army encampment. Films for the Humanities (28 minutes).

To Keep Our Liberty: Minutemen of the American Revolution traces the growing movement toward independence through the eyes of one American patriot. National Park Service Video (35 minutes).

Meet George Washington is a humanizing portrait of Washington as a Virginia planter and colonial businessman who reluctantly assumes a leadership role in the politics of a new nation. Filmic Archives (60 minutes).

Samuel Adams portrays the life and significance of the man who helped create the Sons of Liberty, led the Boston Tea Party, and served in the Continental Congress. Filmic Archives (10 minutes).

Independence, as directed by John Huston, details the dramatic events that led to America's Declaration of Independence in 1776. MPI Home Video (30 minutes).

America: Making a Revolution details the blunders of the imperial government, the increasing colonial agitation for reform, and, ultimately, independence. BBC/Time-Life Video (52 minutes).

Chapter 6
The Revolutionary Republic

CHAPTER SUMMARY

Declaring independence on July 4, 1776, proved to be only the beginning of a great struggle. In the course of the next decade, the American people defeated the British army in a prolonged conflagration, fought loyalists in a civil war, wrote constitutions in each state, and, finally, in 1787 composed the Constitution of the United States.

The Revolutionary War was far longer and more costly than either the Americans or the British could have predicted in 1776. When given a choice, most Indians and most slaves sided with the British. Fighting against the strongest navy in the world and one of Europe's best armies, the American state militias and the Continental Army, led by George Washington, demonstrated exceptional enthusiasm at the beginning of the war. After numerous setbacks during the course of 1776, including the loss of New York City and most of New Jersey, America's "Spirit of '76" began to wane. Only Washington's daring victories at Trenton and Princeton in December 1776 and January 1777 salvaged the campaign and rekindled America's patriotic fervor.

The Revolutionary War dragged on for five more years. In spite of many grave problems, including a hopelessly weak Congress, an ill-prepared, ill-fed, and almost unpaid army and more defeats than victories, American soldiers and civilians persevered. Encouraged by triumphs at Bennington and Saratoga in 1777, the French government formed an alliance with the United States at the beginning of 1778. Within the year, the Spanish had declared war on the British empire as well. Finally, on October 22, 1781, Washington's army forced the surrender of Lord Cornwallis's army of eight thousand men at Yorktown, Virginia, and Lord North's government resigned in early 1782. Within a year, the British recognized American independence by signing the Treaty of Paris. The Revolutionary War was over.

While soldiers were fighting the war, civilians and politicians were constructing new governments in each state. Without the legitimating force of the monarchy, they fell back on the theory of "popular sovereignty." The people themselves, at first through their legislatures, but eventually through constitutional conventions, created the means by which they would govern themselves. The Articles of Confederation, drafted in 1776 and 1777, proved rather ineffectual. Hamstrung by great deficiencies, particularly lack of the power to tax, the Congress proved far too weak; but it did pass the Northwest Ordinance of 1787, which promised that new states would be admitted to the Union as full equals of the original thirteen. When the Constitutional Convention met in Philadelphia in the summer of 1787, the members decided to scrap the Articles entirely. In the ensuing four months, they constructed an entirely new government with vastly increased powers and a system of checks and balances. By creating separate and independent branches of government, by establishing a bicameral legislature, and by staggering elections, the Constitutional Convention created a remarkably resilient balance of liberty and power.

LIBERTY, EQUALITY, POWER: A THEMATIC BRAID

The Revolutionary War taught Americans a great deal. While not everyone learned the same lessons, few came away from the experience without a great respect for the importance of power on the one hand, and a healthy fear of it on the other. That the American people defeated a far stronger British army proved the power of a republican citizenry. Americans had demonstrated their ability to defend liberty. The new challenge was to ensure that no Americans would usurp anyone else's hard-fought liberty. In a nation dedicated to the ideal that "all men are created equal," yet beset by inequality, a new form of government had to be devised. Based on "popular sovereignty," it had to be powerful enough to preserve liberty, while protecting the weak from the powerful at the same time. By 1804, slaves won at least gradual abolition in every northern state.

The solution, the United States Constitution, perfectly satisfied no one. Its composers called it a "great compromise" between big states and small states, slave-holding and free states, East and West, and claimed that it accommodated both central and local power. Some thought it a great mistake, giving far too much power to a central government that would prove to be beyond the ken of all but the most powerful citizens. But for most Americans, the grave weaknesses of the Articles of Confederation convinced them that only greater central power could ensure American liberty. When New Hampshire ratified the Constitution in June of 1788, Americans had created a new government with what promised to be a balance of liberty, equality, and power.

IDENTIFICATIONS

Republicanism
Articles of Confederation
Benedict Arnold
Nathanael Greene
Battle of Princeton
John Burgoyne
Brandywine Creek
Marquis de Lafayette
Battle of Saratoga
Roderique Hortalez et Companie
popular sovereignty
separation of powers
Constitutional Convention
Joseph Brant
King's Mountain
Battle of Cowpens
Robert Morris
Treaty of Paris
coverture
Daniel Boone
three–fifths compromise
New Jersey, Virginia Plans
"necessary and proper" clause
Gnadenhutten
Gordon Riots

Lord North
Northwest Ordinance
Battle of Trenton
Lord Cornwallis
The Howes
Continental Army
Valley Forge
Battle of Bennington
Vergennes
Battle of Springfield
Thoughts on Government
bicameralism
Loyalists
Battle of Camden
Benjamin Lincoln
Impost of 1781
Yorktown
John Carroll
Republican motherhood
Wilderness Road
Daniel Shays
The Federalist
Junípero Serra
Pennsylvania Constitution of 1776
Massachusetts Constitution

Esther de Berdt Reed

Annapolis Convention

Manasseh Cutler

Jay-Gardequi Treaty

CHRONOLOGY

1775	Daniel Boone leads first settlers to Kentucky.
	Virginia Constitution and Bill of Rights.
1776	Declaration of Independence.
	Battles of Long Island and Trenton.
1777	Battles of Princeton, Bennington, and Bemis Heights.
	The Howes take Philadelphia, and Congress flees.
	Burgoyne surrenders at Saratoga.
1778	Franco-American treaties signed.
	Battle of Monmouth Court House.
1778–1781	British offensive in the South.
1780	Massachusetts Constitution.
	Benedict Arnold's treason.
1781	Maryland ratifies the Articles of Confederation.
	Lord Cornwallis surrenders at Yorktown, Virginia.
1782	Resignation of Lord North as prime minister.
1783	Treaty of Paris.
1786	Virginia enacts Jefferson's Statute for Religious Freedom.
	Shays's Rebellion in western Massachusetts.
1787	Constitutional Convention meets in Philadelphia.
	Northwest Ordinance passed by Congress.
1787–1788	*The Federalist* published in New York.
1788	New Hampshire is ninth state to ratify Constitution.

THEMATIC TOPICS FOR ENRICHMENT

1. Assess the authors' statement that the Revolution "was a civil war in its own right" (See p. 206).

2. Define the terms *republicanism* and *popular sovereignty*. How were they manifested in the years of the American Revolution?

3. Why did Americans begin to think increasingly in terms of race in the era of the American Revolution? What was the "first emancipation"?

4. Explain the weaknesses of the Articles of Confederation. Why did the Second Continental Congress create such a weak body?

5. What mistakes did the British make in their attempt to win over the hearts and minds of the Americans during the early stages of the war?

6. Discuss the similarities and differences between some of the state constitutions written during the Revolutionary War. In what ways did Massachusetts redefine constitutionalism?

7. Who was a loyalist and who was a patriot in the American Revolution? Did many people change sides during the war?

8. How did the Continental Congress finance the war?

9. What were the main differences between a "cosmopolitan" and a "localist"?

GEOGRAPHY OBJECTIVES

1. Trace the march of the British troops from New York City to Philadelphia. In what state were by far the most battles of the first three years of the Revolutionary War fought (p. 207)?

2. Trace General Howe and General Burgoyne's planned march from the South and North, respectively. Which states would have been cut off from the rest (p. 207)?

3. Locate the major battles of the war in the Lower South in 1780 and 1781 (p. 222).

4. Explain the tactical error Cornwallis made by stationing his army at Yorktown (p. 227).

5. Which states had western land claims at the time of the Revolution (p. 234)?

SUGGESTED ESSAY TOPICS

1. On what basis did Americans reconstruct authority during the American Revolution? What replaced the power and authority of the monarchy? What new institutions were devised to secure authority?

2. Contrast the Articles of Confederation and the Constitution in terms of liberty and power. Was the Constitution a fulfillment of the Revolution or a reaction to its excesses?

3. In what ways did the movement toward independence transform American life? Be sure to discuss politics, economics, and social issues in your answer.

4. After the middle of the eighteenth century, what options did Indians still have in responding to the encroachment of settlers? How had Indian behavior changed since the Iroquois mourning wars of the seventeenth century?

LECTURE OUTLINE

1. The Revolutionary War was as much a struggle for **hearts and minds** as it was one of competing armies, as the conflict turned on social issues as well as political ones, especially early on in the northern war of 1776–1777.
   a. The **British offensive** of 1776 succeeded in gaining ground and wreaking havoc in New York and New Jersey, but it failed to achieve any decisive advantage.

   (Show Transparency 06-02: Map, Revolutionary War in the Northern States)

   b. The **Trenton-Princeton campaign** proved to be crucial successes for Washington's army, predominantly insofar as it helped keep alive the "spirit of '76."

2. The **campaigns of 1777 and foreign intervention**, particularly of the French after Saratoga, proved to be the turning points of the war.
   a. Despite the **loss of Philadelphia**, the Continental Army continued to fight, even as it could not defend the nominal capital of the nation and as the Continental Congress virtually disbanded.

    b. John Burgoyne's army of 7,800 surrendered to American forces under the command of Horatio Gates at **Saratoga** on October 17, 1777.

    c. **French intervention**, which proved critical to ultimate triumph, came almost immediately after the signal victory at Saratoga.

    d. **Spanish expansion and intervention**, also in the aftermath of Saratoga, greatly assisted the American war efforts, particularly insofar as the Spanish forced the British to spread their forces even more thinly.

3. With the Declaration of Independence and the withdrawal of many **Tories**, Americans faced the uncertain challenge of the reconstitution of authority.

    a. A first attempt to reconstitute legitimate authority came from **John Adams** and his theories in *Thoughts on Government* on the **separation of powers**.

    b. The **Virginia Constitution**, which contained a declaration of rights drafted by George Mason, served as model for others states to follow.

(Show Transparency 06-01: Cartoon, The Federal Edifice, celebrating New York's Ratification of the New Consititution)

    c. More radical than that of Virginia, the **Pennsylvania Constitution** and its unicameral legislature and plural executive never really worked as its framers had envisioned.

    d. John Adams and his colleagues in Massachusetts redefined **constitutionalism**, incorporating a unique system of checks and balances, and submitting its drafted constitution to town meeting for ratification.

    e. A palpable lack of power and a visceral mistrust of central authority plagued the **Confederation** of the states throughout the revolutionary period.

4. The **crisis of the Revolution** in the years 1779–1783 resulted from the fact that the war dragged on at great social and personal cost for more than six years.

    a. The **loyalists** were many in number and often struggled with the fact that they supported British liberty and simultaneously opposed the war.

    b. The lot of **loyalist refugees**, **black and white**, proved harsh, as many thousands emigrated under duress to Nova Scotia and England.

    c. The **Indian struggle for unity and survival** during the war ran the gamut from bitter opposition to England to awesome frontier violence against American troops.

(Show Transparency 06-03: Map, War on the Frontier, 1777–1782)

5. Perhaps the most gruesome events of the Revolutionary War took place during the **British offensive in the South**, which included Clinton's virtual destruction of Charleston, South Carolina.

(Show Transparency 06-04: Map, War in the Lower South, 1780–1781)

    a. The **partisan war** frequently pitted native-born Tories against patriots in vicious confrontations.

    b. The British offensive and the partisan warfare that ensued led to **mutiny and reform** in the ranks of the Continental army, as well as in the militias.

    c. The final stages of the war in 1781 included Cornwallis's ravaging of Virginia, his surrender at **Yorktown**, and subsequent peace negotiations.

(Show Transparency 06-05: Map, Virginia and the Yorktown Campaign)

6. Years of warfare and independence from Britain inevitably led to a **revolutionary society** that few had imagined a decade earlier.
   a. Several of the most profound changes in society were the **religious transformations**, which included increasing religious toleration and the growth of denominationalism.
   b. The fervor of revolutionary sentiment convinced virtually all of the north, and much of the upper South as well, to manumit its slaves in what historians call the **first emancipation**.
   c. The logic of revolutionary ideology also led to marked changes in the life of women and young men that constituted the **challenge to patriarchy**.
   d. Simultaneous with the defeat of the British, a renewed thrust of **western expansion and conflict with Indians** that would take several decades to resolve.
   e. One of Congress's last acts was the passage of the **Northwest Ordinance**, which would ultimately bring Ohio, Indiana, Illinois, and Michigan into the Union on equal footing with the original thirteen states.

   (Show Transparency 06-06: Map, Western Land Claims during the Revolution; and Transparency 06-07: Map, Advance Settlement to 1790)

7. Out of the strains and trials of the decade of revolution, many American called for the wholesale revision of the Articles of Confederation and the creation of **a more perfect union**.
   a. There was no one precipitate of the Constitutional Convention; rather, a combination of problems with commerce, debt, currency, and **Shays's Rebellion** contributed to the growing discontent with the Articles.
   b. The struggle over the government of the Union took the form of a fight between **cosmopolitans versus localists**.
   c. In the course of the summer of 1787, participants at the **Philadelphia Convention** drafted the Constitution, scrapping the Articles altogether.
   d. **Ratification** was confirmed when New Hampshire, the ninth state, voted in favor of the Constitution on June 21, 1788.

   American Album: Toward Equality: The Affectionate Family

   Conclusion: Despite daunting odds and the dangers of what amounted to a civil war, the Americans managed to persevere through years of warfare, economic tribulations, and weak leadership to defeat the British. Imperial ineptitude greatly enhanced the Americans' chances for victory. Victory did not come without significant social upheaval that caused grave problems under the Articles of Confederation.

TEACHING RESOURCES

Abigail Adams discusses the life of this important American in light of the changing attitudes toward women in the era of the American Revolution. Filmic Archives (30 minutes).

Liberty: The American Revolution, volumes IV–VI, offers a broad, well-narrated portrait of the Revolutionary War, with particular emphasis on the military campaigns. PBS Video (55 minutes each).

Valley Forge: The Battle for Survival portrays the events of the fateful winter of 1778 and its larger implications for American independence. Films for the Humanities (23 minutes).

The Battle of Yorktown: 1781 examines the origins of the Revolution, culminating in the British surrender at Yorktown, from a long-term perspective. Films for the Humanities (30 minutes).

Christmas 1783 celebrates America's victory over the British from the perspective of Annapolis, Maryland, where George Washington went to resign as commander in chief before the Confederation Congress. Films for the Humanities (28 minutes).

Fighting for Independence: The Revolutionary War reenacts the major events of the war, political and military, from a number of perspectives. Filmic Archives (20 minutes).

George Mason and the Bill of Rights focuses on the Virginia Ratifying Convention and the debates over the federal Constitution. ETV Video through Social Studies School Service (50 minutes).

Breaking Colonial Ties: Declaration of Independence explains the patriot and Tory viewpoints in Revolutionary America and examines the position of women, slaves, and Native Americans in the debate. Filmic Archives (20 minutes).

Chapter 7
The Democratic Republic, 1790–1820

CHAPTER SUMMARY

The period from 1790 to 1820 was characterized by geographical expansion and economic diversification. The growth of the new nation affected all Americans, as politics and culture changed dramatically. From New England seaports and southern plantations to the Appalachian frontier, America was becoming a democratic republic. Some benefited greatly from these changes, but many did not.

Farmers, artisans, and yeomen, who for so long had felt comfortable with a rough "agrarian republicanism," discovered they were living in a world that was undergoing rapid transformation. Most farmers found themselves increasingly insecure, often maintaining their economic status by having wives and daughters perform outwork of one sort or another. Providing for their children's future became all but impossible. Sons moved away when they could, while daughters were forced to marry much later in life. The growth of overseas trade and the concomitant rise of seaboard towns provided some opportunity for economic independence. Ultimately, achieving a simple "competence" gave way to searching for markets and striving for money.

Society and economy in southern states changed dramatically at the turn of the nineteenth century. Chesapeake farmers moved away from slave labor as they produced foodstuffs, while planters in the rapidly expanding Deep South undertook large-scale production of cotton. The growing English demand for raw cotton and the invention of the cotton gin by Eli Whitney suddenly made cotton planting hugely profitable. Even Thomas Jefferson, who penned the Declaration's "all men are created equal," sold his slaves southward instead of freeing them. While the free black population grew rapidly in the aftermath of the Revolution, the slave population ballooned in much of South Carolina, Georgia, and the new states of the Southwest. Even the admonition of Methodist John Wesley that slavery was a great injustice in the eyes of God failed to slow America's recommitment to slavery.

Nowhere was the growth of the democratic republic more obvious than in the backcountry. Settlers poured through the Cumberland Gap and traversed the National Road into the West. Kentucky and Tennessee followed Vermont as the fifteenth and sixteenth states, while Ohio and Louisiana joined the Union shortly thereafter. With the admission of Maine and Missouri in 1820–1821, America boasted twenty-four states.

LIBERTY, EQUALITY, POWER: A THEMATIC BRAID

The Jeffersonian vision of an America of self-sufficient farmers and artisans never existed. Yet the ideal of "agrarian republicanism" appealed to many Americans in the years after the Revolution. Jeffersonians stressed the grave dangers inherent in all forms of power. The sole adequate means to protect liberty rested with virtuous farmers, artisans, and yeomen, whose freedom and independence enabled them to be good citizens and patriots.

Republicans like Thomas Jefferson vigorously defended equality, particularly in the face of those who stressed the interests of the elite. Yet, republicans restricted equality too, denying rights to many Americans, including free blacks and women. Since independence was essential to gaining equality, only those who owned their own property could be trusted with republican liberty.

While Jeffersonians controlled much of the national government in the decades after independence, they could do very little to secure their vision of America. As president, Jefferson managed to curtail the size of the government and virtually double the size of the nation. His successors did not fare as well. The War of 1812 and the tremendous growth of the economy forced the republicans to abandon their plans for a nation of farmers. Most Americans gradually began to produce for market, simultaneously making themselves more prosperous and less secure.

IDENTIFICATIONS

H. St. John de Crevecoeur
Notes on the State of Virginia
barter/cash
Cumberland Gap
Fallen Timbers
Old Northwest
William Henry Harrison
Tecumseh
Eli Whitney
freehold
Alexis de Tocqueville
Francis Asbury
John Wesley
Saint Dominque

competence
outwork
Agrarian Republicanism
Five Civilized Tribes
Treaty of Greenville
Prophetstown
Tenskwatawa
Battle of Tippecanoe
John Jacob Astor
deism
camp-meeting revivals
Cane Ridge
Gabriel's Rebellion

CHRONOLOGY

1782	Crevecoeur publishes his *Letters of an American Farmer*.
1789	National government commences under the Constitution.
1791	Vermont becomes the fourteenth state.
1792	Kentucky becomes the fifteenth state.
1793	Eli Whitney invents the cotton gin.
	Anglo-French War begins.
1794	Anthony Wayne's Third Army is victorious at Fallen Timbers.
1795	Treaty of Greenville signed.
1796	Tennessee becomes the sixteenth state.
1799	Successful slave revolution in Saint Dominique.
1800	Gabriel's Rebellion in Virginia.
1801	First camp meeting at Cane Ridge, Kentucky.
1803	Jefferson purchases Louisiana from France.
	Ohio becomes the seventeenth state of the Union.
1811	Battle of Tippecanoe.
1812	War of 1812 commences.

THEMATIC TOPICS FOR ENRICHMENT

1. Define the term *competence*. Explain how the goal of competence was distinct from the more contemporary goal of "getting rich."

2. What were the basic beliefs of "agrarian republicanism"? Why was the ownership of property so important in the republican theory?

3. How did the rise of markets change the lives of various Americans from farmers and artisans to frontiersmen and slaves?

4. What were the major factors in the destruction of the Woodlands Indians? Why did "many Indian societies sink into despair"? (See p. 9 in the chapter.)

5. What was meant by the epithet "our white savages"? Who might call a frontiersman by such a name?

6. In what ways did slaves' lives change in the years after American independence?

7. Why might the first decades of the nineteenth century be called the "alcoholic republic"?

8. In what ways did the admission of new states change the meaning of citizenship and suffrage?

GEOGRAPHY OBJECTIVES

1. Sketch the area of land, occupied by 1790, west of the Proclamation Line of 1763 (p. 170, 255).

2. In what territories was most of the Indian fighting concentrated in the years after the Treaty of Paris (p. 251)?

3. Which states were the most densely populated in 1820? Which ones had grown the fastest since 1790 (p. 255)?

4. Name and locate the new slave states that entered the Union between 1790 and 1820 (p. 257).

SUGGESTED ESSAY TOPICS

1. In what ways did the American economy diversify during the first decades of the early republic? Discuss the impact of diversification on the economy of the different regions of the nation.

2. Explain the importance of gender roles in a patriarchal society. How did the role of women and men change in the course of the early republic?

3. In the years after the American Revolution, the country seemed to go in two opposite directions on the issue of slavery. Why did some sections of the country "recommit to slavery," while other regions gradually terminated the institution altogether? Why did Methodists fail in their attempts to spread John Wesley's message that slavery transgressed "all the laws of Justice, Mercy and Truth"?

LECTURE OUTLINE

1. The United States at the turn of the nineteenth century was a **farmer's republic**, composed of a rural people whose lives revolved around community and family. Few Americans lived in metropolitan areas or regularly engaged in market relations.

   (Show Transparency 07-01: Venerate the Plough)

   a. **Households** were more than just the primary social unit, as most production, even that for overseas markets, was done within the household economy.
   b. Most manufacturing was part of what was called the **rural industry**, such as shoe making, quilting, and carpentry, and served the needs of the family first.
   c. **Neighbors** proved especially important as sources of information, exchange, and assistance, as people might not travel much beyond their village in their entire lifetime.
   d. Children still gained the wealth of their parents through **inheritance**, but the institution underwent dramatic changes in the early years of the new republic.
   e. Rising **standards of living** materially improved the lives of many Americans, while also increasing the disparity between rich and poor.

2. Americans flooded out of the East, continuing a constant emigration **from backcountry to frontier** that would last at least a century.

   a. The eventual eviction of the British from the continent, combined with Americans' insatiable appetite for western lands, virtually guaranteed the **destruction of the Woodlands Indians** in only a few decades at the end of the eighteenth and beginning of the nineteenth century.

   (Show Transparency 07-02: Map, Native America, 1783–1819)

   b. Despite the efforts of the likes of Alexander McGillivray, Tecumseh, and the Prophet to articulate some form of Indian **cultural renewal**, Indians could secure no real modus vivendi with the American nation.
   c. While remaining an area largely beyond effective government and organized institutions, the **backcountry** was transformed by the flood of western settlers from 1790 to 1815.

   (Show Transparency 07-03: Map, Population Density, 1790–1820)

3. The **plantation South** underwent a similar transformation, as new settlers and new crops—cotton in particular—changed the character of much of the region from 1790 to 1820.

   a. Despite the first emancipation, **slavery** became increasingly enmeshed in the life of the nation south of the Mason and Dixon Line in the first decades of the nineteenth century.
   b. The upper and lower South made a particularly strong, if unpremeditated, **recommitment to slavery**, particularly after the development of the cotton gin.

   (Show Transparency 07-04: Map, Distribution of Slave Population, 1790–1820)

   c. Nowhere were the issues of **race, gender, and labor** more contested than in the Chesapeake, where the economic transition from tobacco to grain altered many social institutions.

d. The areas of the Deep South where rice and indigo were the primary staples developed a **lowland task system** of slave labor in which slaves gained a significant amount of autonomy as well as separation from white masters.

4. **Seaport cities** grew incredibly swiftly in the years 1790–1815, at the beginning of which only 6 percent of Americans lived in areas with a population over 2,500.
   a. **Commerce**, particularly the trafficking in foodstuffs, fueled the steady growth of the urban centers of the Atlantic seaboard.
   b. **Poverty** was more visible in cities, where slums emerged as the self-contained neighborhood of a growing indigent population.
   c. The **status of labor** changed with the decline of the unique position of artisans, of whom some became owners and far more joined the growing pool of unskilled laborers.

5. The **assault on authority** and the concomitant decline of deference were the characteristic features of the rise of a democratic society, as well as the result of the stratification of the American social structure.
   a. Many contemporaries believed they were witnessing the declension of **paternal power**; children moved away from their homes, and the entire country seemed to celebrate youth.
   b. Americans drank such a high volume of intoxicating beverages that some have called the period the **alcoholic republic**.
   c. Continuing a trend that had commenced in the eighteenth century, the **democratization of print** in the early republic was unmistakable, particularly the rise of literacy and the proliferation of newspapers.
   d. **Citizenship** remained the province of white males but expanded greatly to include virtually all white men, especially in the new western states.

6. Americans embraced a form of **republican religion** that in many ways reflected the democratization of the polity.
   a. The most important feature of republican religion was the decline of tax-supported **established churches**, with only Massachusetts holding out until 1833.
   b. The **rise of the democratic sects**, Baptists and Methodists especially, reflected Americans' desire to have as much choice and freedom in religion as in other walks of life.

   (Show Transparency 07-05: Map, Growth of American Methodism, 1775–1850)

   c. The **Christianization of the white South** featured great camp revivals and the simultaneous growth of black and white denominations of Baptists, Methodists, and others.
   d. **Evangelicals and slavery** maintained a tenuous relationship, with evangelicals ultimately remaining subservient to the economic interests of the plantation South.
   e. The first decades of the nineteenth century witnessed the beginnings of **African-American Christianity** and religious institutions in which blacks maintained autonomy from the dominant white society.
   f. **Gabriel's Rebellion** was brutally subdued in the summer of 1800, but nonetheless expressed a unique version of **black republicanism**.

American Album: Revival at York, Pennsylvania

Conclusion: The Americans who celebrated the beginning of national government in the 1790s were overwhelmingly a rural people. Yet, these same folks comprised a nation in the midst of many changes that would usher in a more individualistic, acquisitive republic in the years to come. Transformations in the cultural life of the country clearly reflected the economic ferment of the period.

TEACHING RESOURCES

Lewis and Clark: The Journey of the Corps of Discovery is Ken Burns's rendition of the most famous American expedition of the nineteenth century. PBS Video (120 minutes each).

A Few Men Well-Conducted: The George Rogers Clark Story tells the epic story of courage on the frontier and the trek into the Kentucky and Illinois backcountry in the era of the American Revolution. Filmic Archives (23 minutes).

Settling the Old Northwest details the dynamics of settlement and socialization in the lands between the Ohio and Mississippi Rivers. Filmic Archives (18 minutes).

Thomas Jefferson: The Pursuit of Liberty attempts to give a balanced portrait of the man and his ideas. It explores the complex life of the man who simultaneously held slaves and authored the Declaration of Independence. Thomas Jefferson Memorial Foundation Video (38 minutes).

Awakening Land, based on the Conrad Richter trilogy, details the story of life on the Ohio frontier. PBS Video (108 minutes).

Chapter 8
Completing the Revolution, 1789–1815

CHAPTER SUMMARY

When Robert Livingston swore in George Washington as America's first president on April 30, 1789, the American people had much to celebrate. They had won the war, secured independence, adopted a new government, and unanimously elected Washington their leader. Still, as the president well understood, there was much to be done to complete the Revolution.

The first Federalist administration, together with the first Congress, boasted some of the country's best and brightest. Complementing the president were Vice President John Adams of Massachusetts, Secretary of State Thomas Jefferson of Virginia, and Treasury Secretary Alexander Hamilton of New York. Consciously playing the role of president of a large and diverse nation, Washington assiduously sought to foster unity within the government. He judiciously distributed patronage to men from every state and himself made a tour of the North. Unanimously elected to a second term, Washington proved only marginally successful at keeping himself above factional disputes. No sooner had Hamilton issued his comprehensive economic reports, which included federal assumption of state war debts, funding the government's liabilities at 100 percent, and the creation of a national bank, than a fierce opposition emerged in the cabinet and in Congress. With the president's backing, Hamilton pressed ahead with his vision of a strong central government, while his opponents, coalescing around Jefferson and James Madison, fought vigorously against what they considered a travesty of the narrow language of the Constitution. When Washington retired at the end of his second term, he warned in vain against the dangers of party spirit and its potential for splitting the country.

Foreign affairs plagued the administration of John Adams. The French Revolution and the ensuing Anglo–French War split the country down the middle. President Adams heeded Washington's warning about foreign entanglements. He ignored the advice of the Democratic-Republicans, who sympathized with France, as well as those in his own Federalist Party, who urged him to declare war on the French. Through the XYZ Affair, the quasi-war, and the Alien and Sedition Acts controversy, Adams managed to keep the young nation at peace. Staying out of the war, in the end, irreparably damaged the Federalist Party as well as the president's political fortunes. Adams became the first chief executive to lose his bid for reelection.

Historians have called Jefferson's defeat of Adams the "Revolution of 1800." Not only was the campaign ferociously fought between rival parties with new electioneering techniques, but the election itself marked the first time in history that power was transferred peacefully. Adams and the Federalists were not entirely confident that Jefferson would not destroy the Republic, but they well understood that he had been legally and constitutionally elected president. With the ouster of Adams, the Federalists were forced to rely on John Marshall, newly appointed Chief Justice of the Supreme Court, to preserve federalism in Washington.

Jefferson's policies as president reflected for the most part his vision of a small government in a large agrarian republic. Accordingly, he shrank the size of the bureaucracy, slashed spending for the standing army and navy, and, in one bold stroke, doubled the size of the nation. The Louisiana Purchase, while a heavy-handed executive motion, proved to be Jefferson's most important act as president. For $15 million, the president secured America's future as an "empire of liberty."

Like his predecessor, Jefferson found himself embroiled in foreign policy. At once curtailing the nascent United States navy, the president pursued an uncompromising policy toward both England and France. While nonimportation proved a failure and the 1807 embargo a fiasco, Jefferson did manage to leave office with the country at peace. His successor was not so fortunate. The War of 1812, derisively called "Mr. Madison's War" by New Englanders, accomplished little besides getting the nation's capitol burned by the British. The Treaty of Ghent effectively ended the war where it had started, but for the Federalist debacle at the Hartford Convention and the emergence of Andrew Jackson, the hero of the Battle of New Orleans. Although the battle was fought more than two weeks after the war had ended, Jackson emerged as America's first prominent national figure who had not been associated directly with the Revolution. As a result of the War of 1812, the Democratic-Republicans vanquished the Federalists, but at a price. In fighting a great conflagration, they reluctantly had adopted most of their opponent's policies. Protecting liberty required the use of power.

LIBERTY, EQUALITY, POWER: A THEMATIC BRAID

Completing the Revolution, most Americans agreed, required the creation of a new national government. The Constitutional Convention created a government with vastly greater powers than those enjoyed by Congress under the Articles of Confederation. Yet, no sooner was George Washington inaugurated president, than deep divisions appeared between those who felt the Constitution set the limits of central power and those who considered the Constitution a blueprint for expanded governmental action. In the early Republic, the century-long fight between power and liberty continued under the new guise of Federalist versus Democratic-Republican.

Federalists believed that power ensured liberty. Accordingly, they sought to engage the government actively in creating a powerful commercial republic, based on internal economic development, overseas trade, and a navy strong enough to defend American interests. If these actions entailed a loose construction of the Constitution and reliance on the "necessary and proper" clause, then so be it.

Republicans, including James Madison, the "father of the Constitution," feared power in anyone's hands. They were convinced that Federalists would come to abuse central power just as the British, whom their opponents emulated, had done in the decades before the Revolution. For Republicans, completing the Revolution meant ensuring liberty through a bill of rights, strict construction of the Constitution, and a vigilant stand against their power-hungry opponents. Ironically, Republicans and Federalists agreed on the meaning of equality. Americans were hardly equal, nor should they be. Equality was reserved solely for those independent members of society who had a visible financial stake in the country. This proved to be a minority of predominantly white males.

IDENTIFICATIONS

Federalist Party	Democratic-Republicans
precedent	James Madison
Bill of Rights	Judiciary Act of 1789
presidential cabinet	Alexander Hamilton
John Jay	report on public credit

Bank of the United States
strict construction
Citizen Genêt
Jay's Treaty
Pinckney's Treaty
The Directory
quasi-war with France
Virginia and Kentucky Resolves
Jacob Fries
midnight appointments
District of Columbia
John Randolph
Marbury v. *Madison*
"empire of liberty"
Non-Importation Act
Fort Mims Massacre
Chesapeake-Leopard affair
Battle of the Thames
Hartford Convention

Whiskey Rebellion
French Revolution
orders in council
impressment
farewell address
XYZ Affair
Alien and Sedition Acts
High Federalists
John Marshall
Aaron Burr
Louisiana Purchase
Yazoo Land Company
Haiti
Napoleon Bonaparte
Berlin, Milan Decrees
War Hawks
Francis Scott Key
Oliver Hazard Perry

CHRONOLOGY

1789	Washington inaugurated as first president of the United States in New York City.
	Judiciary Act establishes a Supreme Court.
1790	Report on Public Credit delivered to Congress.
	Bill of Rights drafted by Congress.
1792	French Republic proclaimed.
1793	Anglo–French War.
1794	Whiskey Rebellion.
1796	Jay's Treaty and Pinckney's Treaty ratified.
	Washington delivers his farewell address.
1798	XYZ Affair.
	Undeclared war between the United States and France.
	Alien and Sedition Acts passed by Congress.
1799	Slave revolution in Haiti.
1800	Washington, D.C., becomes American capital.
	Republican Jefferson defeats Fedcralist Adams.
1803	Louisiana Territory purchased from France.
	Marbury v. *Madison* case.
1804	Twelfth Amendment to the Constitution.
1806	Non-Importation Act.
1807	Chesapeake–Leopard affair.
	Congress passes Jefferson's Embargo Act.

1810	Macon's Bill No. 2.
1811	Henry Clay elected Speaker of the House.
1812–1814	War of 1812.
1814	Hartford Convention.
	Treaty of Ghent.
1815	American victory in the Battle of New Orleans.

THEMATIC TOPICS FOR ENRICHMENT

1. What were the different titles suggested for the American president? Why did the debate prove so vitriolic?

2. Who was likely to be a Federalist? A Democratic-Republican?

3. List the specific liberties guaranteed in the Bill of Rights.

4. Explain the main points of Hamilton's economic plans.

5. Who were the members of Washington's first cabinet? What were their home states?

6. Assess Hamilton's and Jefferson's views on the constitutionality of the Bank of the United States.

7. Explain why the Jeffersonians sympathized with France and the Federalists sided with England in the 1790s.

8. What were the warnings Washington delivered in his farewell address?

9. What were the Virginia and Kentucky Resolves written in response to? What was the basic principle behind them?

10. What was so important about New Orleans that Jefferson insisted that the United States gain control of the city?

11. Why did virtually all Federalists in the twelfth Congress vote against going to war with England in 1812? Assess the Federalist claim that the conflict was solely a "war of territorial aggression."

GEOGRAPHY OBJECTIVES

1. On a map of the United States in 1790, mark off the home states of the members of Washington's first cabinet (p. 285).

2. Identify the states that voted Republican and those that voted Federalist in the presidential election of 1800 (p. 291).

3. Mark on a map the major battles of the War of 1812 (p. 304).

4. Find the three United States capitals between 1789 and 1800 (p. 304).

SUGGESTED ESSAY TOPICS

1. In what ways did the fight between the Federalists and the Democratic-Republicans echo the Revolutionary contest between liberty and power?

2. What did Jefferson mean in his inaugural address of 1801 when he claimed that "we are all Republicans, we are all Federalists"? Assess the importance of the "peaceful transit of power" after the election of 1800.

3. Did Thomas Jefferson live up to his own political ideals of less government and "strict constructionism" during his two terms in the presidency?

4. Compare the foreign policies of the Federalists and those of the Republicans. Which were more effective?

5. Read "Federalist #10" by James Madison and answer the following questions: What is it about? Has the Constitution succeeded in checking the danger of majority factions as the author believed it would?

LECTURE OUTLINE

1. **Establishing the government** with the ability to tackle the economic and political problems was the first priority of Washington, his administration, and the first Congress.
   a. The Washington administration had to struggle with the irony of appearing to create a **"republican court"** of powerful appointed officials in a democratic society.
   b. Leadership in the **first Congress** fell to James Madison, under whose guidance the Congress pursued a course to strengthen central authority in order to counteract questionable state actions.

   (Show Transparency 08-01: The Congressional Brawlers, 1798)

   c. The cornerstone of the first Washington administration was the system of **Hamiltonian economics** that would come to grips with the national debt, begin to regulate the currency, and foster economic expansion.
   d. Several aspects of the plan of Hamiltonian economics came under fire, particularly the proposals for the **bank and the excise**.
   e. The **rise of opposition** was inevitable, as southerners especially felt that Hamilton's plans favored the mercantile interests of the North.
   f. The beginnings of party politics stemmed from the growing rift between Washington's two principal advisors in the cabinet, **Jefferson and Hamilton.**

2. Foreign policy concerns often cast a shadow over domestic concerns as the nation's political leaders differed greatly in their views on the **Franco-English War** from 1793 to 1800.
   a. Most Americans initially considered the **French Revolution** to be a significant step toward a republican world, but Federalists soon came to view the events in France with skepticism, fear, and dismay.
   b. **Citizen Genet**, as French minister to the United States in 1793, conspicuously intervened in American internal affairs.
   c. The Washington administration faced acute **western troubles**, the Whiskey rebels in particular, in the course of 1794, ultimately sending a army of 12,000 men to quell the so-called rebellion.

   (Show Transparency 08-02: Map, Securing the West, 1790–1796)

d. Vehemently opposed by many, the **Jay Treaty** helped the United States avert war with England while settling many issues left unresolved in the Revolutionary War settlement.

e. In September 1796, newspapers printed **Washington's Farewell**, in which the chief executive announced his retirement and offered several admonitions about politics and foreign policy.

f. John Adams, the heir apparent, narrowly defeated Jefferson in the **election of 1796**, winning New England and several of the middle states.

g. **Troubles with France** plagued Adams's entire administration, overshadowing virtually all of Adams's domestic initiatives.

h. The struggle with France and England turned into a **crisis at home from 1798 to 1800** especially when the Federalist Congress passed the Alien and Sedition Acts and the Kentucky and Virginia legislatures sought to nullify them within their state boundaries.

i. Politicians fought heatedly over the nature of the appropriations for, future size of, and leadership of the **United States Army**.

j. Styled the "revolution of 1800" by the victorious Jefferson, the **election of 1800** marked the first defeat of an incumbent administration as well as the peaceful transit of power.

3. Making good on their campaign pledges, the **Jeffersonians in power** immediately sought to curtail the pomp and ceremony that was so prominent in the previous administration.

a. While it continued many of the features of its predecessors, the **Republican program**, articulated by Jefferson, Madison, and Albert Gallatin, sought to shrink the activities of the central government and to eliminate altogether the national debt.

b. **Cleansing the government** meant for Jefferson the removal of his partisan opponents while shrinking the size and scope of government.

c. The greatest disputes of the administration proved to be between the **Jeffersonians and the courts**.

   i. Jefferson personally sought the **impeachments of Pickering and Chase** for a combination of partisanship and gross dereliction of duty.

   ii. **Justice Marshall's court**—and Chief Justice John Marshall himself—proved to be Jefferson's greatest challenge, particularly after Marshall's Solomon-like decision in the case of *Marbury* v. *Madison* in 1803.

d. Jefferson secured his legacy and his reelection with the remarkable purchase of **Louisiana** from the French in 1803 for the paltry sum of fifteen million dollars.

(Show Transparency 08-03: Map, Louisiana Purchase)

4. Republican attention for many years remained riveted on the emerging crisis between the Republic and its involvement in the **Napoleonic Wars** between 1804 and 1815.

a. Jefferson and Madison understood the daunting **dilemmas of neutrality** in a world at war but had a great deal of difficulty convincing New Englanders that neutrality should be maintained at all costs.

b. The Republicans desperately tried to steer clear of the **trouble on the high seas** created by both British and French naval depredations and the British practice of impressing American sailors into service on his majesty's ships.

    c. Jefferson sought to avoid war in the last years of his presidency by the passage of the **embargo** which proved extremely unpopular in New England.

    d. Jefferson's retirement and the failure of the embargo seemed to send the country inevitably down the **road to war** with Great Britain.

    e. Led by Henry Clay of Kentucky, the **Warhawk Congress of 1811–1812** wanted war with England in order to eliminate Britain's Indian allies in the West.

    f. Despite Washington's earlier warning and Jefferson's attempts at economic coercion, the United States all but backed into the **War of 1812.**

    (Show Transparency 08-04: Map, War of 1812)

      i. Early skirmishes included a failed northern invasion as part of the bloody **War with Canada in 1812-1813** that included depredations on both sides.

      ii. **Tecumseh** made his last stand at the Thames River on October 5, 1813, where Richard M. Johnson claimed to have fatally wounded the warrior.

     iii. The **British offensive of 1814** concluded with the humiliating sacking of the nation's capital.

     iv. A group of disgruntled Federalists gathered at the ill-fated **Hartford Convention** in order to publicly protest against "Mr. Madison's War."

      v. The war officially ended with the signing of the **Treaty of Ghent** on December 23, 1814, although news did not arrive in New Orleans until after Andrew Jackson's smashing victory over General Packenham's army.

American Album: The Capital of the Republic

Conclusion: Almost all of the founding generation agreed that the stronger national government ushered in by the Constitution was essential to American prosperity and security; nonetheless, fissures shortly developed between those who advocated an activist government and those who contended, with Jefferson, that "he who governs best, governs least."

TEACHING RESOURCES

Thomas Jefferson is Ken Burns's fine two-part examination of the third president, with Sam Waterston reading Jefferson's words. PBS Video (180 minutes total).

United States vs. Aaron Burr recreates the trial of Burr, the one-time vice president of the United States. Educational Video (60 minutes).

The Life of George Washington features Bill Bradley narrating a detailed portrait of the first president of the United States. Filmic Archives (32 minutes).

City Out of the Wilderness: Washington details the founding of the American capital at the end of the eighteenth century. Filmic Archives (30 minutes).

Virginia Plantations focuses on two of Virginia's most famous homes, Monticello and Mount Vernon. Filmic Archives (30 minutes).

Marbury v. *Madison*, one tape in the *Equal Justice Under Law* series, explains this 1803 Supreme Court case and its significance for American jurisprudence. PBS Video (30 minutes).

Mr. Jefferson and His University examines the originality of Jefferson's vision through an examination of the University of Virginia and several of his other achievements. Films for the Humanities (52 minutes).

Chapter 9
The Market Revolution, 1815–1860

CHAPTER SUMMARY

The conclusion of the War of 1812 ushered in a new economic era. Between 1815 and the coming of the Civil War, the United States underwent a furious economic transformation. The primary engines of this great expansion of the United States's economy proved to be a revolution in transportation and the subsequent burgeoning of a market economy. Jefferson's republic of independent farmers became, in the course of several decades, a market-oriented capitalist society.

It is ironic that the Republican-dominated Fourteenth Congress devised the nationalistic programs that helped to subsidize the market revolution. In 1816, Congress chartered the Second Bank of the United States. It also enacted a protective tariff that raised rates an average of 25 percent and passed several bills to provide federal money for roads, canals, and other internal improvements. Although Congress never embraced Henry Clay's "American System" in its entirety, the Republican government assumed a significant share of the burden for improving the nation's transportation system.

Both states and private investors contributed ideas and capital to the transportation revolution. New York entrepreneur Robert Fulton launched the first steamboat in 1807. In the ensuing years, a proliferation of steamboats enabled farmers to make their way speedily back upriver after selling their products. What formerly was a two- to three-month trip from New Orleans to Louisville or Cincinnati became a pleasant ten-day river ride by 1850.

The Erie Canal turned out to be the greatest single achievement of the transportation revolution. Built between 1817 and 1825, the 364-mile canal connecting the Great Lakes to New York City generated huge profits for its investors, turned upstate New York wilderness into highly desirable farmland, drew many New Englanders and immigrants westward, and enabled New York to live up to its billing as the Empire State. Eventually displaced by the railroads, the Erie Canal remained the crowning achievement of the early years of the transportation revolution.

The Federalists had long held that federal power could ensure the growth of a market economy. John Marshall, as the sole Federalist in a prominent position in the national government at the time, used the Supreme Court to prove the Federalists right. In a series of court cases, Marshall established the supremacy of the federal government, ensured the sanctity of charters and contracts, and set interstate commerce above the regulation of the individual states. By the time Marshall retired in 1835, the Supreme Court had guaranteed that the United States would enjoy the benefits of a national economic system.

By far the most important result of the market revolution proved to be the steady rise in material standards of living. Improved transportation, lower freight costs, expanded overseas markets, and the rise of a cash-based economy all contributed to American prosperity. Still, the market revolution did not come cheap. Many people failed to prosper in the generally improving national economy while others systematically were excluded from enjoying the ever-increasing profits from their labors. As cotton production and profits boomed in the South, more and more slaves suffered from the arduous demands of the cotton economy. When the price of slaves increased, fewer Chesapeake slave-holders freed their slaves. In no small measure, the first manumission ended with Eli Whitney's invention of the cotton gin. The market revolution did not signal the end of slavery.

LIBERTY, EQUALITY, POWER: A THEMATIC BRAID

Liberty, equality, and power are not solely functions of governmental and legal action. Economic factors have proven at least as important in American progress toward greater personal liberty and equality. The market revolution provided a tremendous opportunity for Americans to stake their claim to the ideals of the American Revolution and independence. Material standards of living rose in the years after the War of 1812.

Yet not everyone benefited equally. Some grew wealthy, others improved their lives somewhat, and still others found themselves adversely affected by the growth of American capitalism. Transportation usually proved critical. For those Americans who could farm, mine, build, or otherwise produce items for a market, fortunes generally improved, occasionally dramatically, in the course of the first half of the nineteenth century. For those who found themselves unable to produce anything for a market, few economic opportunities appeared. Without skills or capital, many Americans joined a growing class of workers and laborers, who, but for the slaves, occupied the lowest station in society.

In sum, then, as the United States became a world economic power, the material wealth of its citizens grew apace. With prosperity came more opportunity and financial freedom. Yet, the nation did not become a land of equality of opportunity. The market revolution proved a mixed blessing. As American wealth increased, so did the distance between rich and poor. By the middle of the nineteenth century, Jefferson's idealistic vision of an egalitarian society of free farmers and artisans was buried under a burgeoning capitalist society.

IDENTIFICATIONS

Treaty of Ghent	Battle of New Orleans
Second Bank of the United States	"American System"
John C. Calhoun	Tariff of 1816
internal improvements	National Road
Dartmouth College v. *Woodward*	Erie Canal
McCulloch v. *Maryland*	*Gibbons* v. *Ogden*
Baltimore and Ohio Railroad	Lancaster Turnpike
Robert Fulton	DeWitt Clinton
Natchez Trace	Main Line Canal
cash–crop business	Peter Cartwright
McCormick reaper	Farmer's Almanac
Richard Arkwright	Boston Associates
Frederick Law Olmsted	

CHRONOLOGY

1790	Samuel Slater constructs Arkwright spinning mill at Pawtucket, Rhode Island.
1801	John Marshall was made Chief Justice of Supreme Court.
1807	Robert Fulton launches the *Clermont* on its maiden trip.
1813	Boston Associates built first mill in Waltham, Massachusetts.

1815	End of the War of 1812.
1816	Congress charters Second Bank of the United States.
	Dartmouth College v. *Woodward.*
	McCulloch v. *Maryland.*
	Revised protective tariff passed by Congress.
1818	National Road completed as far west as Wheeling, Virginia.
1819–1825	New York builds Erie Canal between the Hudson River and Buffalo.
1822	President Monroe vetoes National Road reparations bill.
1824	*Gibbons* v. *Ogden.*
1828	Baltimore and Ohio Railroad begins full operation.
1835	Main Line Canal connects Philadelphia and Pittsburgh.

THEMATIC TOPICS FOR ENRICHMENT

1. What was Henry Clay's "American System"?

2. Explain the specific legal results of the three Marshall decisions handed down between 1816 and 1824.

3. What was so important about the invention of steamboats for American transportation in the early republic?

4. Why was the transportation revolution so important to the opening of a market economy in early America?

5. Was any one region of the country mostly excluded from the burgeoning national market system?

6. Evaluate the role of the plantation on the economic development of the South.

7. In what ways were New England farmers adversely affected by the market revolution?

GEOGRAPHY OBJECTIVES

1. Trace the route of the Erie Canal across New York. From how far inland could goods be transported by water to New York City after the completion of the canal (p. 317)?

2. Through which states did the National, or Cumberland, Road make its way (p. 317)?

3. Find the path of the "Natchez Trace" north from New Orleans through Mississippi (p. 317).

4. Compare the rates of travel from New York City to points inland in 1800 and 1830 (p. 320).

5. In which sections of the country were the greatest miles of railroads laid (p. 321)?

6. Contrast the regional growth of cotton in 1801 and 1859 (p. 335).

SUGGESTED ESSAY TOPICS

1. In what ways did the market revolution shatter Jefferson's vision of an agrarian republic?

2. What was the transportation revolution? Discuss the main features of its development between 1815 and 1860.

3. How did the decisions of the Marshall Court demonstrate Marshall's conviction that "a natural and beneficial link exists between federal power and market society"?

LECTURE OUTLINE

1. The party of Jefferson changed dramatically in the years after his retirement. Republicans increasingly agreed that **government and markets** must work closely together to foster economic expansion.

   a. Henry Clay's **"American System"** included the recharter of the formerly dreaded **Bank of the United States** in 1816 over the objections of a number of reactionary Republicans led by **John Taylor of Carolina**.

   b. **"The American System"** incorporated an elaborate system of **tariffs and internal improvements** that expressed Clay's belief that the government must be used for progressive purposes.

   c. Politicians and lawyers sought to assure the effective interaction of **markets and the law**, as reflected in a series of important Marshall court decisions.

2. The **transportation revolution** proved critical to national economic development because the price of many commodities depended more on the costs associated with transporting them to market than to that of production.

   a. The means of **transportation** had not changed very dramatically for many years; a rudimentary system of roads barely supplemented river travel.

      i. Technology and changes in law resulted in dramatic improvements in **roads and rivers** as means of transportation.

      ii. Improvements in **canals and railroads** augured a wholesale change in the means of transport in the United States, despite their high cost.

   (Show Transparency 09-02: Map, Rivers, Roads, and Canals, 1825–1860)

   b. The transportation revolution resulted in a dramatic reduction in the **time and money** it took to transport bulk commodities.

   c. Improved transportation also meant the growth of specific **markets and regions** in an economy of scale.

3. The advent of cash markets ushered in the transformation from **yeoman to businessman**, particularly in the rural North and West.

   a. Cash-oriented farms proved instrumental in shaping the **northern landscape**, as farmers sought to exploit urban demand for perishable crops.

   b. The **transformation of rural outwork** toward more market-oriented production had consequences for both the economy and for society in general.

   c. With the shift to specialized market agriculture, much of the North and West witnessed the growth of **farmers as consumers**.

   d. The Northwest became home to many **southern migrants** who rejected slavery but maintained strong ties to southern cultural traditions.

   e. The Northwest was also the destination of myriad **northern migrants** who rapidly embraced agricultural improvements in order to maximize their cash-crop harvests.

   f. No institution changed more dramatically than **households**, which shifted from economic production to raising fewer children and preparing them for a career outside the home.

     g. New neighborhoods designed as a **landscape of privacy** ushered out the old practices and forms of neighborliness characteristic of communities where everyone knew one another.

4. **The Industrial Revolution** commenced in New England in the 1830s and 1840s.
   a. Factory towns under the **Rhode Island system** emerged as a result initially of the espionage of Richard Arkwright, who stole English plans.
   b. Factory towns under the **Waltham system** employed young women in their mills, exploiting this readily available source of cheap labor.
   c. Cities featured the growth of a class of **urban businessmen**, who used their wealth and position to dominate much of urban society.
   d. **Metropolitan industrialization** sparked the development of a new middle class that made the old distinction between proprietor and dependent obsolete.

5. Proponents of the **market revolution in the South** centered their appeal around westward expansion and the world's seemingly insatiable demand for cotton.

   (Show Transparency 09-03: Map, Cotton Production, 1801 and 1859)

   a. The huge profits from cotton planting necessitated the **organization of slave labor**, including the use of women in the fields and the encouragement of slave families.
   b. Planters used a system of **paternalism**—caring for slaves as more than commodities—to ensure that the supply of slaves would not wane and to discourage the most vicious treatment of blacks.
   c. With the economies of scale brought about by cotton production, southern society was increasingly differentiated into **yeomen and planters**.
   d. Planters generally mediated the relationship of **yeomen and the market**, functioning as factors, lenders of labor, and advisors.
   e. **Plantations and southern development went hand in hand**; the southern economy grew rapidly, albeit narrowly, as planters churned profits back into land and slave labor.

   American Album: The Making of Rural Respectability

   Conclusion: Despite the fact that the Jeffersonians attempted to foster an agrarian republic of yeomen farmers, the War of 1812 and the strength of the American economy forced the Republican party to adapt. Under Jefferson and Madison, Republicans endorsed many of the programs and initiatives that they had condemned under their Federalist predecessors. The nation was undergoing a transformation that signaled a burgeoning capitalistic market revolution.

TEACHING RESOURCES

Remaking Society in the New Nation examines the struggles of two men who make their way in the early years of the American republic. Filmic Archives (21 minutes).

The Louisiana Purchase: Moving West of the Mississippi highlights the politics and culture of the newest settlements of turn-of-the-nineteenth-century America. Filmic Archives (16 minutes).

Settling the Old Northwest depicts the conflicts that arose between aggressive western settlers and the Native American tribes between the Ohio and Mississippi Rivers. Filmic Archives (18 minutes).

Gone West exposes the harsh realities of life on the western frontier in the eras of Jefferson and Jackson. BBC\Time-Life Video (52 minutes).

Chapter 10
Toward an American Culture

CHAPTER SUMMARY

New territories, the market revolution, and the continued spread of plantation slavery produced wave after wave of social change in America after 1815. New social patterns replaced or changed old ones, often as a consequence of religious revival. Americans remained primarily devoted to Protestantism, capitalism, and republican values, but the emerging northern middle class interpreted these matters differently than did the plantation owners of the South. Northern urban workers, farmers, and free blacks defined these values differently both from their southern counterparts and from one another. From these differences there emerged an American range of subcultures created by religion, region, class, and race.

The new wave of evangelism launched by revivalists such as Charles Grandison Finney stressed individual salvation and social reform in order to trigger the millennium, a thousand-year reign of Christianity that would precede the Second Coming of Christ. The northern middle class that responded to the evangelicals' crusade used this religious goal to create a culture based on a greatly altered family structure and community moral reform.

Middle-class evangelism forever altered the American domestic arena. Gender determined the sphere of work to be done: Men went out of the home to work in markets and finance; women maintained the household and feminized domestic life, assuming most of the child-rearing duties. In the sentimental literature that accompanied and exalted this domestic alteration, mothers became lay evangelicals, who embodied correct Christian living and passed moral values on to their children.

Farmers, laborers, and other "plain people" of the North, in contrast, spurned middle-class optimism and reformism and maintained their simple faith in Providence. Many came to believe that Christ's Second Coming was at hand and found signs of this in nature's storms, eclipses, and shooting stars, as well as in man-made economic catastrophes. William Miller's predictions in the 1830s and 1840s convinced thousands that the world was about to end.

Concern that the patriarchal family was collapsing played a major role in the teachings of Joseph Smith. In the Book of Mormon, patriarchy is the ideal family organization and the villains are selfish merchants, lawyers, and evil priests. The Church of Jesus Christ of Latter-Day Saints, which Smith founded in 1830, established a lay hierarchy of adult males that ran the institution and ensured that believers continued to turn to a patriarchal government for the family and the community.

Greatly disturbing to the religious subcultures was the rise of a largely urban popular culture that revolved around young unmarried males. These men formed militia units, volunteer fire companies, and similar organizations that glorified drinking, boasting, and physical exploits. Blood sports such as cockfighting, dogfighting, and boxing attracted them. New entertainments in theaters drew them as well, where the boisterous, sometimes violent, patrons demanded coarse American drama filled with melodramatic themes, rather than the usual staid fare. The most popular of these theatrical offerings was the minstrel show, where performers in blackface poked fun at black dialect and folkways. Cheap novels and the "penny press" entertained the same patrons with lurid accounts of murder, mayhem, and sexual misconduct.

Meanwhile, white southerners remained localistic and culturally conservative. With a strong sense of family history, they fiercely guarded the traditional family structure and their own roles in it. Honor and reputation were everything, with the code of honor maintaining rigid distinctions between men and women, whites and blacks. "Southern life was not about freedom, individual fulfillment, or social progress; it was about honoring the obligations to which one was born."

By 1860, southern church members were overwhelmingly Methodists, Baptists, or Disciples of Christ. A wave of revivalism at the beginning of the century stressed individual conversion more than social reform, and local control of religious matters rather than denominational directives. Churches thus became the most important institution in southern communities and controlled the moral life of their members much more than did the local government.

In this social structure revolving around religion, family, and fixed social roles, slaves sought a better place for themselves. Their most prized privilege was to make and maintain a family; their greatest fear was separation from the family. Beyond the family, Christianity gave some slaves a sense of themselves as a historical people who, someday, would be delivered from bondage. America was the new Egypt, and Moses was the biblical figure most admired.

For some southern blacks, Christianity offered apocalyptic promises that led to revolt and a violent end to slavery. Denmark Vesey's planned revolt in 1822 equated Charleston with Jericho and South Carolina with Egypt, and in Nat Turner's 1831 revolt, Turner's religious visions served as a means to recruit fellow rebels and as a justification for slaughter.

LIBERTY, EQUALITY, POWER: A THEMATIC BRAID

Power for the northern middle class increasingly became attached to the conversion of others—not only to Christianity, but to their moral code. Moral reform became the means to achieve this power. For southern plantation owners, power meant not change, but the maintenance of the traditional family and the patriarchal class structure that separated men from women and whites from blacks. For the urban working class, power lay in the creation of their own organizations—volunteer fire companies and sporting clubs, for example—and the expansion of a crude, boisterous popular culture. Slaves in the South found few ways to exercise power except through the rare slave revolt.

Liberty and equality for whites in the North and South remained a racial prerogative based on republican values formulated in earlier eras. For white women, a measure of power and equality came with domesticity and sentimentalism, where the female sphere defined by the home gave women more autonomy and greater social importance as the child raisers, moral teachers, and guardians. With the father absent more and more from the home, the mother's importance to the family greatly increased.

IDENTIFICATIONS

Middle class	evangelicalism
Charles Grandison Finney	"blood sports"
Sunday schools	sentimentality
millennialism	minstrel show
Lydia Maria Child	Ralph Waldo Emerson
Nathaniel Hawthorne	Herman Melville
penny press	Walt Whitman
Harriet Beecher Stowe	Charles Colcock Jones

Uncle Tom's Cabin   Denmark Vesey
Niagara Falls   Quaker City
Thomas Cole   Nat Turner
southern code of honor   Joseph Smith
Seventh-Day Adventists   camp meeting
Book of Mormon   William Miller

CHRONOLOGY

1822	Denmark Vesey slave revolt plans exposed in Charleston, South Carolina.
1828	Alexander Campbell debates Robert Owen on religious piety in Cincinnati, Ohio.
1830	Charles G. Finney leads religious revival in Rochester, New York.
	Joseph Smith publishes the Book of Mormon and founds the Church of Jesus Christ of Latter-Day Saints.
1831	Mount Auburn Cemetery opens in Boston.
	First minstrel show is presented.
	Nat Turner's slave revolt breaks out in Virginia.
1835	Landscape artist Thomas Cole publishes "Essay on American Scenery."
1836	Emerson begins writing career with publication of *Nature*.
1837	Hawthorne publishes his first collection of stories, *Twice-Told Tales*.
1843–1844	William Miller converts thousands to the belief that the world is about to end.
1845	George Lippard's lurid novel *Quaker City* becomes a huge best-seller.
1849	Theater riot in New York City leaves twenty dead.
1851	Melville publishes *Moby–Dick*.
1852	Harriet Beecher Stowe's antislavery novel *Uncle Tom's Cabin* is published to great popularity and controversy.
1853	Henry David Thoreau's *Walden* appears.
1856	Whitman publishes first editions of *Leaves of Grass*.

THEMATIC TOPICS FOR ENRICHMENT

1. How did the northern middle class's perceptions of Christianity differ from those of the "plain people"?

2. Explain the rise of domesticity and sentimentalism. How did women benefit from the new definition of their roles?

3. Discuss the changes in Americans' appreciation of the fine arts. How did their view of nature change?

4. Define the "popular culture" that arose among unmarried, urban males in the early decades of the century. What role did immigrants play in this transformation?

5. Discuss the religious beliefs and social philosophy of southern plantation owners and their families.

6. Discuss how southerners used Christianity to justify the enslavement of blacks.

GEOGRAPHY OBJECTIVES

1. Compare the growth of cities north of the Mason-Dixon Line with that of the southern states (p. 317).

2. Find the locations of the Denmark Vesey affair and the Nat Turner rebellion (p. 335).

3. Locate the birthplaces of Emerson, Hawthorne, Thoreau, Melville, and Whitman (p. 285).

SUGGESTED ESSAY TOPICS

1. Define the term "middle class" and discuss the factors that led to its growth in the early nineteenth century.

2. What is a religious revival? In what ways did religion figure into the lives of Americans?

3. What were the key features in the development of American literary culture in the decades before the Civil War?

4. Compare and contrast the cultures of the North and the South.

5. Explain the slave interpretation of religion and family. Did Christianity help or hamper slaves in dealing with their condition?

LECTURE OUTLINE

1. A great development of the first part of the nineteenth century was the advent of a distinct **northern middle class** of Protestant business-oriented folk who came to dominate northern culture.
   a. Members of the middle class not only attended church regularly but also emerged from a solid **evangelical base** of Christian revivalism.
   b. The **cult of domesticity** resulted from the middle class distinction between home and work, with the latter the exclusive provenance of men.
   c. The popular literature of the class, such as *Gody's Ladies Book*, featured effusive **sentimentality** directed primarily at women.
   d. Americans slowly came to view the **fine arts** as something that could take on a non-European, indigenous character.
   e. American artists' unique contribution to fine arts was the incorporation of **nature and art**, especially in the work of the Hudson River School of painting.
   f. **Scenic tourism** became a special American form of entertainment, with **Niagara Falls** as one of the country's most popular destinations.

2. **The plain people of the North** rejected much of the sentimentality and evangelicalism of middle-class values, pursuing their own distinct forms of culture.
   a. The **religion of the common folk** proved far less sentimental and far more participatory than that of the well-heeled and the middle class.
   b. **Popular millennialism**, particularly that of William Miller and the Millerites, looked forward to God's imminent arrival to redeem the saved.
   c. Some religious ideologies appealed to the notions that **family and society** must be counterposed against encroaching and immoral market forces.
   d. The **prophet Joseph Smith**, after the angel Moroni appeared to him in a vision in 1827, articulated a version of American Protestantism known as Mormonism.

3. Coterminous with the profusion of religious institutions came the **rise of popular culture**.
   a. **Blood sports** such as cockfighting, ratting, and dogfights proved highly popular with the urban working class.
   b. Prizefighting, or **boxing**, grew out of subterranean culture to become a highly popular form of entertainment throughout society.
   c. Americans of all stripes overcame the old Puritan squeamishness and began to patronize an **American theater**, which featured everything from Shakespeare to amateur spectacles.
   d. The most popular form of theater was the **minstrelsy**, which demonstrated the blatant racism of most of America.
   e. Among the many commodities the market revolution made available, few were more ubiquitous than **novels and the penny press**, which included sales of millions of cheap books and magazines.

4. The leading elements of southern whites self-consciously built their society around the three pillars of **family, church, and neighborhood**.
   a. The individualism of northern culture proved secondary to the place of **southern families,** and southern honor, in the values of the South.
   b. **Southern entertainments**, including horse racing, hunting, fishing, and other outdoor activities reflected the essentially rural character of the South.
   c. As more southerners found religion a form of entertainment as well as a source of spiritual nourishment, the **camp meeting** became respectable.
   d. Southerners embraced **religious conservatism** together with a conviction that fundamental political and social traditionalism was vital to its culture.
   e. In time, the union of plantation economic interests and Protestantism resulted in a distinctly **proslavery Christianity**.

5. Determined to shield themselves from their masters in some measure, slaves sought to maintain distinctly **private lives**, often at great personal risk.

   (**Show Transparency 10-01: 1849 Handbill Offering $600 Reward for 3 Runaway Slaves**)

   a. The **slave family**, a vital element in the difficult rigor of slave life, emerged as a crucial institution separate from white oversight, at least to some extent.
   b. In spite of events like Nat Turner's Rebellion, **white missions** resulted from southern evangelical preachers' abandonment of their hostility toward slave religiosity.
   c. **Slave Christians** embraced the evangelism but ignored much of the secular teachings of the white missionaries, who sought to use religion as a means of assuring slave submissiveness.
   d. Invariably, **religion and revolt** came together in the violent insurrections of Denmark Vesey in South Carolina and Nat Turner in Virginia.
   e. **Nat Turner** led a rebellion in 1831 that forced Virginians to reconsider the institution of slavery in the Old Dominion.

American Album: P. T. Barnum's American Museum

Conclusion: In the wake of the changes that accompanied the market revolution, a distinct set of American cultural values emerged, although with distinct differences north and south of the Mason and Dixon Line. Adherence to republican values and a wholesale embrace of market capitalism characterized the new culture of the northern middle class, while southerners were more reticent about embracing market forces.

TEACHING RESOURCES

Harriet Beecher Stowe: Uncle Tom's Cabin offers an abridged version of the George Aiken dramatization. Films for the Humanities & Sciences (45 minutes, color).

The West, episode two, examines the early, yet steady expansion of Americans into the West. PBS Video (55 minutes).

Working for the Lord discusses the impact of religion on the lives of eighteenth- and nineteenth-century Americans. Republic Pictures Home Video (52 minutes).

Chapter 11
Society, Culture, and Politics, 1820s–1840s

CHAPTER SUMMARY

By the 1840s, the Whig and Democratic Parties had well-defined constituencies. In the North and West, Whigs drew the support of merchants, factory owners, native-born factory workers, artisans, and middle-class evangelists. Whigs pushed for government action to accelerate the market revolution and to promote a moral code that involved Sabbath observance, temperance, and Bible-based schools. In the South, Whigs shared their northern colleagues' support for economic development but shunned their program for government-backed moral reform.

Democrats received the backing of cultural traditionalists, both from the North and South: farmers from areas bypassed by the market revolution and religious groups ranging from Irish Catholics in the cities to Baptists, Methodists, and Disciples of Christ in the South. The latter groups supported individual moral reform but rejected government interference in moral matters.

In the politics of social reform, both parties agreed that government should support common schools. Differences arose, though, over control. Whigs sought state-level centralization of schools; Democrats called for self-control for each local school district. Whigs wanted a state-imposed uniform curriculum; Democrats wanted a cheaper, locally controlled alternative.

In the movement to reform criminals, Whigs pushed for prisons that emphasized rehabilitation. They felt that a prison's controlled setting would provide inmates with work and discipline and would turn them into good citizens. Most Democrats viewed rehabilitation with skepticism and wanted prisons to punish criminals for their antisocial behavior. The Auburn Prison system, a compromise between the two camps, became the legislature's favorite.

By the 1820s and 1830s, reform movements of a bewildering variety swept through the nation. With the founding of the American Society for the Promotion of Temperance in 1826, the most popular reform of the era emerged. To assault the nation's alcohol problem, local, state, and national temperance organizations formed. Temperance, abstinence, and, finally, state-imposed prohibition drew reformers' support. With the formation of the Washingtonian Society in 1840, reformed drunkards contributed to the movement as well.

Race relations changed dramatically in the same era. While most northern and southern whites remained committed to white superiority over blacks, a minority of northern whites eventually embraced antislavery. For free blacks in the North, a new wave of European immigrants threatened their economic position and helped to create hostilities that led to race riots in Philadelphia and New York City. Democratic ideologues charged that blacks were not fit to be citizens in the white man's republic; Whigs offered lukewarm support for black citizenship.

Abolitionists from 1831 onward rejected the gradual emancipation and repatriation schemes of the American Colonization Society and demanded an immediate end to slavery and full civil and legal rights for blacks. Abolitionism thus became the most controversial reform of the era. Despite enormous opposition from both political parties, abolitionists brought the slavery question to the public arena and recast the debate over slavery into terms of political power and civil liberties.

Women, particularly those from a northern middle-class evangelical background, found power of a kind in the reform movements. Using their newfound role as protector of family values, women launched a crusade to reform prostitutes and to curb male sexual excesses. Through their work in the abolition movement, many women perceived the need for women's rights. Beginning around 1840, they lobbied state legislatures and achieved rights to own property, earn their own wages, and take custody of children in divorce cases. At the Seneca Falls convention in 1848, women activists began their quest for the right to vote.

LIBERTY, EQUALITY, POWER: A THEMATIC BRAID

Equality became a goal in the 1830s and 1840s for a significant portion of American women. Engendered in large measure by their experience in the moral reform and abolitionist movements, women rejected the concept of separate spheres for males and females, and they insisted that each individual, male or female, should be allowed to achieve his or her full potential. At their women's rights meetings, they began the pursuit of suffrage rights that would last several decades.

For white men, power continued to be sought in economic opportunity and political development. For those who enthusiastically embraced the market revolution and who wanted the government to promote more internal improvements, banks, schools, and moral restraint, the Whig Party became the means to these ends. For those who supported the new economic order but still held deep suspicions about excessive government involvement in the economy and in private life, the Democrats were the party of choice.

For free blacks in the North, political power and equality remained elusive. Their economic power even declined in these two decades as they faced economic competition from the Irish and other immigrants. Their social position declined, and antiabolitionist sentiment and political demagoguery erupted in the form of race riots. For enslaved blacks, growing support for the abolitionist movement by whites and blacks alike meant that the morality of slavery was now in question to a degree never seen before in the nation. The abolitionists' promise of racial equality after the demise of slavery became a goal—and a dream—that all blacks could endorse.

For middle-class evangelists, liberty and equality before God could be pursued best through a many-faceted reform crusade. The millennium would arrive when Christian Americans, aided by their government, eliminated ignorance, alcohol, Sabbath-breaking, prostitution, sexual excesses, and other vices. Schools and prisons would form and reform, respectively, the character of the young and the criminal.

IDENTIFICATIONS

Democratic Party	Whig Party
Horace Mann	American Anti-Slavery Society
New York Herald	Sojourner Truth
Auburn system	Sylvester Graham
George Bancroft	William Seward
Philadelphia system	John Humphrey Noyes
Native American Party	Female Moral Reform Society
Dorothea Dix	New York Magdalen Society
American Temperance Society	The Advocate of Moral Reform
Washington Temperance Society	Sarah Grimke
American Colonization Society	Women's Rights Convention

The Liberator   William Lloyd Garrison
Fifteen-Gallon Law   Daniel Webster
                                              Wendell Phillips

CHRONOLOGY

1816	African Methodist Episcopal Church forms in Philadelphia.
	American Colonization Society created to send blacks to Africa.
1819	Prison reform system implemented at Auburn, New York.
1826	Reformers set up American Society for the Promotion of Temperance.
	Lyman Beecher publishes sermons against alcohol.
1828	New York Magdalen Society founded.
1829	New York Safety Fund law passed.
1830	Alexis de Tocqueville tours the United States.
1831	William Lloyd Garrison's *The Liberator* begins publication in Boston.
	New York Magdalen Society's report on prostitution shocks the city and launches the moral reform crusade.
1833	Abolitionists found the American Anti-Slavery Society.
1834	Antiabolition mob sacks the house of abolitionist Lewis Tappan in New York.
	First major race riot breaks out in Philadelphia.
1835	American Anti-Slavery Society commences postal campaign agitation.
1838	Massachusetts legislature passes Fifteen-Gallon Law.
1840	Washington Temperance Society forms as an organization for reformed drunkards.
1844	Native American Party wins New York City elections.
1848	First Women's Rights Convention held in Seneca Falls, New York.
1860	New York State passes Married Women's Property Act.

THEMATIC TOPICS FOR ENRICHMENT

1. What issues united southern and northern Whigs? What issues divided them?

2. Discuss the banking situation in the United States after the destruction of the Second Bank of the United States.

3. What were the differences between Whigs and Democrats in their plans for public education?

4. Why were Catholic parents upset with public schools and determined to establish church-controlled schools?

5. Discuss the differences between the Philadelphia System and the Auburn System for prison reform.

6. Which social reform of the era did the South support most enthusiastically? Why?

7. Describe the different ways that temperance reformers tried to curtail the consumption of alcohol.

8. What was the response of free blacks to declining economic, political, and social conditions in the 1830s and 1840s?

9. What caused the race riots of the 1830s in Philadelphia and New York?

10. How did abolitionists during this period differ from antislavery advocates that had come before them?

11. Describe the reform efforts of the Female Moral Reform Society.

12. What was the link between abolitionism and the women's rights movement?

GEOGRAPHY OBJECTIVES

1. What states comprised the Old Northwest (p. 285)?

2. On a map of North, Central, and South America, identify Haiti, Mexico, Peru, Chile, and Colombia (p. 35).

3. Find Liberia and its capital, Monrovia, on a map of Africa (p. 11).

SUGGESTED ESSAY TOPICS

1. Contrast the Whig and Democratic parties of the 1830s and 1840s. Who were their respective leaders and constituents, and what were their ideologies?

2. Compare that first party system of Federalists and Republicans with the second party system of Whigs and Democrats.

3. Define "social reform" and discuss its many goals in the 1830s and 1840s.

4. Explain the relationship of religion and politics in the second party system.

5. Characterize the life and struggles of free blacks in antebellum America.

LECTURE OUTLINE

1. As politics became more institutionalized, politicians had to compete for specific **constituencies**, largely based on region and class.
   a. The North and West, dominated by commercial farmers and enterprising immigrants, became the key locus of support for the emerging **Whig Party**.
   b. Planters and yeomen of the South almost uniformly turned out a majority for the **Democratic Party** and its intransigent stance against national regulation of slavery.

2. The **politics of economic development** were played out in the two-party rivalry of Democrats and Whigs, with the differences between the parties often proving more rhetorical than real.
   a. No issue was more central to the parties than that of the nature of **government and its limits**, with the Whigs arguing for more forceful and imaginative use of the central power.
   b. Like Jefferson's Republicans, Jackson's Democrats believed **banks** were of dubious morality.
   c. The Whigs, and Henry Clay in particular, contended that **internal improvements** fostered economic growth, and therefore should be funded by the federal government.

3. Members of both major parties, as well as the many lesser ones, fought vociferously over **social reform**, especially as it became clear that reform issues proved critical in elections.
   a. Far from being universally acclaimed, **public schools** became a prominent feature, and a large public expenditure, solely in the North and Northwest.
   b. For many locally minded citizens, the mixture of **ethnicity, religion, and the schools** was so volatile that party affiliation became a passionate issue even in small towns.
   c. State investment in **prisons** grew dramatically in the period, with some states following the Pennsylvania system and others following the "Auburn system."
   d. States also funded the construction of **asylums** to house orphans, the insane, the dependent poor, and criminals.
   e. Cultural and political conservatism inhibited the South from taking similar positive steps on **social reform** as had the North.

4. The **politics of alcohol** was so great an issue that in many regions the temperance question constituted the difference between Whig and Democrat.
   a. The fight to prohibit **ardent spirits** became the obsession of many Americans, who started temperance organizations such as the American Temperance Society.

   (Show Transparency 11-01: The Drunkard's Progress)

   b. The **origins of prohibition** were rooted in New England, where Massachusetts passed a "Fifteen-Gallon Law" in 1838.
   c. The **democratization of temperance** stemmed from the increasing willingness of citizens to vote according to their views on ardent spirits.
   d. Whig disapproval of the Washingtonians' tactics led to a series of **temperance schisms** in the 1840s.
   e. By the 1850s and the immigration of many **Irish and Germans** whose culture included drinking, ethnicity and alcohol became the focus of political and social discord.

5. When it had become clear that slavery was not about to disappear of its own accord, the **politics of race** became increasingly contentious, threatening to divide almost all institutions along the Mason and Dixon line.
   a. One peculiar result of slavery and racism was the anomalous condition of the increasing numbers of **free blacks** in both the North and South.
   b. Rampant **discrimination** against blacks and immigrants was endemic in the United States before the Civil War.
   c. While discrimination was ubiquitous in antebellum America, **democratic racism** served to encourage a systematic attempt to equate American citizenship solely with white Protestantism.
   d. Antebellum America featured an entire community of pseudoscience that espoused a number of pernicious **conceptions of racial difference**.
   e. The **beginnings of antislavery** dated to years prior to the American Revolution, but most antislavery advocates believed that the end of slavery would necessitate the colonization of blacks.
   f. **Abolitionists** believed that slavery was a sin, and as such it had to be removed immediately, not gradually.
   g. Copying other reformers, abolitionists began to use various active forms of **agitation** to raise consciousness of the treatment of slaves.

6. With the discussions of racial slavery came similar debate over women's rights, which resulted in a new **politics of gender and sex**, culminating in the Seneca Falls Convention of 1848.

    a. Numbers of different reform groups sought to curb dangerous and licentious **appetites**.

    b. **Moral reform**, through organizations such as the New York Magdalen Society, was proposed as a means to improve society through nonpolitical avenues.

    c. From the 1820s onward, middle-class women began the century-long struggle toward **women's rights** and the American woman suffrage movement.

American Album: The Bulwark of the Republic

Conclusion: The society, culture, and politics of the decades of the 1820s, 1830s, and 1840s incorporated changing attitudes toward family, religion, race, class, ethnicity, and more. As the United States became an increasingly democratic, aggressive nation, America's cultural institutions adapted to serve the ideological needs of a people on the move.

TEACHING RESOURCES

"Harriet Tubman" and "Sojourner Truth" are video biographies in the twelve-part *The Black Americans of Achievement* video collection. Filmic Archives (30 minutes).

The Freedom Station is a drama about the Underground Railroad that is set in a "safe house" in 1850. It explores the concept of freedom versus the reality of being free. Filmic Archives (30 minutes).

Mr. Lincoln of Illinois re-creates the era and the man in this documentary about Lincoln during his prairie years. Films for the Humanities & Sciences (30 minutes, color).

Elizabeth Cady Stanton and Susan B. Anthony examines the lives of the women's rights pioneers. Films for the Humanities & Sciences (24 minutes, color).

Roots of Resistance details the story of the Underground Railroad in graphic, compelling terms. PBS Video (60 minutes).

Chapter 12
Jacksonian Democracy

CHAPTER SUMMARY

Jacksonian Democracy arose in great measure from reactions to the Missouri crisis of 1819 and the economic recession of the same year. In both the North and South, political leaders began to reconstruct the limited-government, states' rights coalition that had defined Jeffersonian republicanism. By 1828, this coalition would become the new Democratic Party.

When the Missouri crisis revealed the South's commitment to slavery and the North's growing resentment of the South's political power, political realignment began in earnest. The simultaneous collapse of the market economy further divided the political groups, as some now blamed the banks for the collapse. Others defended the banks and the economic structure that they had made possible. Political realignment gained momentum with the election of 1824, when four presidential candidates emerged from the old Republican Party.

By 1828, Andrew Jackson's wing of the Republican Party was becoming the Democratic Party. Charging that the nation had gone astray because of selfishness, greed, and "corrupt bargains," Jackson called for a return to government by the Democratic majority. John Quincy Adams's version of republicanism, according to Jackson, called for excessive government spending, high taxes, government intrusion into private matters, and special privileges for the economic elite. The presidential campaign, filled with mudslinging propaganda from both camps, brought Jackson and his new party into power.

As an example of his states' rights commitment, Jackson allowed the southern states to declare sovereignty over Native American lands within their boundaries and pushed for removal of the tribes to the West. His commitment to nationalism, however, resulted in his clash with South Carolinians over nullification of the Tariff of 1828. In Jackson's mind, a state's right to nullify federal legislation was tantamount to disunion; disunion was not a right, but an act of treason.

In economic matters, Jacksonians championed the producing classes over the privileged elite, even making war on the Second Bank of the United States on their behalf. To Jackson, the bank was a government-sponsored concentration of power and privilege. Jackson's opponents saw the bank as a stabilizing force and a necessary institution for economic expansion.

By 1834, Jackson's opponents had converted Adams's and Henry Clay's "national republicanism" into the Whig Party. Martin Van Buren and the Democrats continued the Jacksonian ascendancy in 1836, but in the 1840 campaign, the Whigs and William Henry Harrison emerged as a national party that successfully challenged the Democrats and gained the presidency. The new two-party system that had been forming since 1819 was now complete.

LIBERTY, EQUALITY, POWER: A THEMATIC BRAID

How to acquire power—more than liberty and equality—was the question for the generation of the 1820s and 1830s. Beginning with the Missouri crisis, southern leaders saw any attempt to stop slavery's expansion as an attempt to limit southern political power. Northern leaders, indeed, viewed the expansion of the slave trade as the South's quest for more political power.

For Andrew Jackson and the Democratic Party, power had been lost to those who pushed for banks, paper money, and other financial complexities in the market economy. The Second Bank of the United States was the worst usurpation of power yet. Also a great danger, the Jacksonians believed, was the growing power of the federal government, as it spent more money on internal improvements, raised taxes, and catered to the privileged. John Quincy Adams, Henry Clay, and their kind, Jacksonians charged, were betraying the republic to greed, corruption, and elitism.

For southern radicals such as John C. Calhoun, even the Democrats' support of states' rights was not enough to protect South Carolina from the federal government. Other sections of the nation, they feared, already had too much power that could affect the South's economic and political future. Only the right to nullify federal actions could save a state's liberty.

In the ongoing struggle for territory in Georgia and other southern states, Native Americans and whites sought the favor of the federal government. Native Americans wanted to retain sovereignty and asked merely that the federal government uphold its treaties; whites asked for sovereignty over all land within state boundaries and wanted tribal claims abolished.

For most Americans, equality still meant white equality. Jacksonians carried the issue into the political arena, charging that political or social systems differing from theirs challenged this equality.

IDENTIFICATIONS

Sacajewea	Meriwether Lewis and William Clark
Sioux	Talmadge Amendments
Missouri Compromise	Arkansas Territory
Nat Turner	Force Bill
Panic of 1819	gag rule
John Quincy Adams	Peggy Eaton
Second Bank of the United States	Nicholas Biddle
Era of Good Feelings	Specie Circular
Martin Van Buren	Bank Veto Message
William Crawford	Pet Banks
King Caucus	Independent Treasury Bill
American System	Panic of 1837
"Corrupt Bargain"	Whigs
"Spoils System"	"Tippecanoe and Tyler Too"
Adams-Onís Treaty	Log Cabin Campaign
Worcester v. *Georgia*	Trail of Tears
(Five) Civilized Tribes	Denmark Vesey conspiracy
Tariff of 1828	nullification
Calhoun's Exposition and Protest	

CHRONOLOGY

1804–1806	Lewis and Clark expedition explores upper Louisiana and crosses the Continental Divide.
1816	Congress charters Second Bank of the United States.
1819	Panic of 1819 marks first failure of the national market economy.
	Crisis arises over Missouri's admission to the Union.
	Adams-Onís Treaty extends American border to the Pacific Ocean.

1820	Missouri Compromise adopted.
	Maine becomes the twenty-third state.
1821	Missouri becomes the twenty-fourth state.
1822	Denmark Vesey conspiracy uncovered in South Carolina.
1823	Monroe Doctrine written by John Quincy Adams.
1824–1825	Adams wins presidency over Andrew Jackson.
	Adams appoints Henry Clay Secretary of State.
	Jacksonians charge "corrupt bargain" between Adams and Clay.
1827	Cherokees in Georgia declare themselves a republic.
1828	Jackson defeats Adams for presidency.
	"Tariff of Abominations" passed by Congress.
	John C. Calhoun's Exposition and Protest presents nullification doctrine.
1830	Congress passes Indian Removal Act.
	Marshall hands down verdict in case of *Cherokee Nation* v. *Georgia*.
1831	Nat Turner's rebellion extinguished in Virginia.
1832	"Bank War" erupts in Washington politics.
	Jackson reelected over Henry Clay.
	Worcester v. *Georgia* favors Cherokees in jurisdiction dispute.
	Jackson vetoes bill to recharter the Bank of the United States.
1833	Force Bill and Tariff of 1833 end the nullification crisis.
1834	Whig Party formed.
1836	House of Representatives adopts "gag rule" to table abolitionists' petitions.
	Martin Van Buren elected president.
1837	A severe economic depression begins with the Panic.
1838	"Trail of Tears" begins as army force marches Cherokees to the Indian Territory.
1840	Whig William Henry Harrison defeats Van Buren for the presidency.
	Congress passes Independent Treasury Bill.

THEMATIC TOPICS FOR ENRICHMENT

1. How did the North and the South react to Missouri's petition to enter the Union?

2. Discuss the causes of the Panic of 1819. What role did banks play in this recession?

3. Who were the presidential candidates in 1824? What did each have to offer to the voters?

4. Discuss Andrew Jackson's background, character, and political philosophy.

5. How did John Quincy Adams differ from Jackson in regard to background and political philosophy?

6. Discuss the 1828 election in terms of the issues and the propaganda that each put forth.

7. Describe the Indian-removal issue from either the point of view of the Georgia government or from the point of view of the Cherokees.

8. Explain John C. Calhoun's nullification doctrine and why it was opposed by Andrew Jackson.

9. Discuss the Bank War from the viewpoints of Andrew Jackson and Nicholas Biddle.

GEOGRAPHY OBJECTIVES

1. Divide the United States into approximate regions: New England, Chesapeake, Deep South, Middle States, Northwest, and Southwest (p. 408).

2. Plot the expedition of Lewis and Clark up the Missouri River. Identify the locations of the various Indian tribes mentioned in the chapter (p. 439).

3. Find on a map the Missouri Compromise line of 36 degrees, 30 minutes. Identify free and slave states (p. 437).

4. Sketch the United States's southern border after the Adams-Onís Treaty of 1819 (p. 431).

SUGGESTED ESSAY TOPICS

1. Compare Andrew Jackson's political career and his views on government with those of Thomas Jefferson.

2. Explain the impact of the Missouri debates on the politics of the Jacksonian era. Why did Thomas Jefferson call the controversy "a fire-bell in the night"?

3. Define the term *nationalism*. In what ways is nationalism a positive characteristic for a people? In what ways is it a negative one?

LECTURE OUTLINE

1. The year **1819** was a volatile one in the United States as debates over Missouri statehood and the bank panic set the stage for tumultuous events in the subsequent two decades.
   a. The **West** from 1803 to the 1840s was a land of bold exploration, methodical settlement, and wild stories of Indians, endless deserts, and impassable mountains.
   b. Congress was almost paralyzed by sectional arguments over **Missouri statehood** and the fate of slavery in the West.
   c. Congress averted disaster with the passage of the **Missouri Compromise**, which made Missouri a slave state and Maine a free state, as well as established a northern boundary for the expansion of slavery in the Louisiana Purchase territory.
   d. The **Panic of 1819** caused the collapse of many banks and brought economic depression to many regions of the nation.

2. Events of 1819 and 1820 led to a **Republican revival**, with virtually all national political figures seeming to call for small government, sectional peace, and government noninterference in slavery.
   a. New Yorker **Martin Van Buren** led the way toward the construction of a new, more modern political party, known as the Jacksonian Democratic Party.
   b. The **election of 1824** proved a fiasco with none of the four candidates garnering an electoral majority, thus throwing the election into the House of Representatives.

    c. Henry Clay's support of John Quincy Adams and his subsequent appointment to the post of Secretary of State led to wide-scale accusations that a **"corrupt bargain"** had been struck between Clay and Adams.

    d. Between 1825 and the next election, a veritable **Jacksonian melodrama** ensued, in which Jackson's men publicly lamented their candidate's unfair denial of the nation's highest office.

3. The nation found itself in the midst of the **rebirth of sectionalism** under the guise of two highly contentious personalities, Jackson and Adams.

    a. The **Adams-Onís Treaty** and the promulgation of the **Monroe Doctrine** moved American nationalism to a much larger international arena.

    b. **Nationalism at home**, while getting a big boost from Adams's educational and scientific initiatives, failed to take root in a Congress and public that remained wary of central power.

    c. The **birth of the Democratic Party** stemmed directly from the public persona of Andrew Jackson and the behind-the-scenes machinations of Martin Van Buren.

    d. Jackson's victory in the **election of 1828** vindicated the general and demonstrated the power of Van Buren's emerging party machine.

    e. Sympathetic contemporaries called Jackson's March 4, 1828, inauguration, a **people's inauguration**, while skeptics viewed it as a display of the debauchery of the common folk.

    f. Contemporaries termed Jackson's open replacement of government appointees with his own political operatives the **spoils system**.

4. Elections from the 1820s to the Civil War demonstrate the crucial ties of **Jacksonian Democracy and the South**.

    a. Simmering tensions between southerners and Indians, whose land claims proved anathema to expansionists, turned to open conflict in large measure with Jackson's explicit approval and his public disavowal of the Supreme Court's decision in the case of *Worcester* v. *Georgia*.

    b. The official government policy known as **Indian Removal** was predicated upon the almost reflexive assumption that white and red could not live in harmony.

    c. One constant from Jefferson to Jackson proved to be **Southern opposition to the tariff**.

    d. Ostensibly in response to artificially high tariff rates, South Carolinian John C. Calhoun promulgated the doctrine of state **nullification** of national law.

    e. The dispute over the reputation of Secretary Eaton's wife among the wives of Jackson's Cabinet resulted in the **"petticoat wars"** that split the Administration between Peggy's attackers and defenders.

    f. The Eaton affair and the publication of the vice president's criticism of Jackson's actions during the Seminole War led to the **fall of Calhoun**.

    (Show Transparency 12-01: "Despotism" Cartoon Showing Calhoun Reaching for the Crown)

    g. The sectional dispute over slavery erupted around Congress's debate over petitions, the **gag rule**, and the southern mails.

5. **Jacksonian democracy and the market revolution** ultimately went hand in hand, as aggressive nabobs and the nouveaux riches sought political power to displace entrenched elites.

     a. Supporters of rechartering the **Second Bank of the United States** came together to form the Whig Party at the beginning of the 1830s.

     b. When the president vetoed the Second Bank's rechartering bill, a **bank war** ensued as the "monster bank" became the central issue of the 1832 presidential campaign.

     c. The **beginnings of the Whig Party** date from the bank war and Jackson's heavy-handed and highly personal style of governance.

     d. Jackson's supporters enthusiastically endorsed a **balanced budget** as a means to ensure that the government remained relatively small and unobtrusive.

6. The birth of the Whigs and the consolidation of the Jacksonian Democrats brought about the **second American party system**.

     a. Jackson's inflationary bank policies led to the Panic of 1837 and made the reelection of **"Martin Van Ruin"** a virtual impossibility.

     b. The patently crude political machinations of both Whigs and Democrats in the **election of 1840**, such as dispensing of massive quantities of hard cider, were caricatured throughout the emerging popular press of the day.

     c. Despite the shenanigans, the election of 1840 ensured the success of an American electoral system driven by **two parties**.

American Album: Log Cabins and Hard Cider

Conclusion: Despite Jacksonian nostrums about minimal government, the economic growth, territorial expansion, and remarkable immigration of the 1830s and 1840s forced both political parties to actively pursue control of the national government to accomplish their highly political ends. Echoing the sentiments of the Jeffersonians, the Democratic Party proved far more adept at winning national office than their Whig opponents.

TEACHING RESOURCES

When the White Man Came briefly describes life among the major tribes across the United States at the time of European arrival. Films for the Humanities & Sciences (13 minutes, color).

The Trail of Tears focuses on white expansion and the impact on Native American cultures. Films for the Humanities & Sciences (13 minutes, color).

Journals of Lewis & Clark re-creates with live action scenes of the journey along the Missouri River. Filmic Archives (60 minutes).

Gone West examines the myths and realities of nineteenth-century life on the frontier. BBC /Time-Life Video (52 minutes).

Andrew Jackson: A Man for the People is the best portrait of the American president, Indian fighter, and symbol for an age. Arts and Entertainment Video (50 minutes).

Chapter 13
Manifest Destiny:
An Empire for Liberty—or Slavery?

CHAPTER SUMMARY

The near doubling of the nation's size in the 1840s gave credence to the concept of Manifest Destiny. Many Americans believed that Providence's grand design was for the United States to occupy all of North America. Intertwined with this was the racist belief that Native Americans, Mexicans, and anyone else who might stand in the way of expansion would be expelled. However, the question of slavery's role in this grand design still remained unanswered.

By the 1840s, the Oregon Country drew expansionists' attention. Oregon's discovery by "mountain men" and missionaries created a land rush known as "Oregon fever." At the same time, the Oregon Country became a source of contention between the United States and Great Britain.

Elsewhere, the westward march brought the Mormons under Brigham Young's leadership to arid lands around the Great Salt Lake. In territory still claimed by Mexico, Mormons sought isolation and self-determination in order to prevent clashes with their non-Mormon neighbors that had plagued the group in the East.

As the decade continued, traders and would-be settlers moved into New Mexico and California, sparking expansionist interest in these lands. At the same time, Texans, independent since 1836, agitated for annexation to the United States. James Knox Polk and the Democrats' victory in the 1844 election seemed a clear mandate for occupation of all the coveted territories: Oregon, New Mexico, California, and Texas.

In his first two years in office, Polk welcomed Texas into the American fold, split the Oregon Country with Great Britain, and offered to buy California and the rest of the Southwest from Mexico. Failing in the latter effort, Polk found pretexts for war with Mexico to achieve by conquest what negotiations had not produced.

The Mexican War deeply divided the nation, in large part because it brought into sharp focus the question of slavery's expansion. Deeply distrustful northerners saw Texas's annexation and the Mexican conflict as a territorial "grab" by the slave-owning southerners. Those same southerners, such as John C. Calhoun, saw the Wilmot Proviso and the Free Soil stance as efforts to contain the South and to destroy its political power. Seeking a middle position, supporters of popular sovereignty, such as Lewis Cass and Stephen A. Douglas, tried to make the issue of slavery's expansion a matter of territorial policy and not one of national debate that threatened to split North from South.

California's acquisition from Mexico and the almost simultaneous discovery of gold there deepened the growing rift between the two sections. By the end of 1849, with Californians clamoring for statehood, with Texas bitterly disputing the boundary with New Mexico, with abolitionists trying to rid the nation's capital of slavery, and with proslavery supporters agitating for a harsher fugitive-slave law, the Union faced its greatest crisis to date. With the Compromise of 1850, the question of slavery's expansion was settled in regard to California but remained unanswered in other areas, including possible new territories in the Caribbean and Central America. Meanwhile, the Compromise's Fugitive Slave Act, an ill-disguised proslavery effort to force northerners to show more support for slavery, brought mob action against slave catchers and federal officials trying to enforce the law. The publication of *Uncle Tom's Cabin* and other regional protests seemed a rallying cry for northern whites, who saw the slave trade as a threat to their own civil liberties.

LIBERTY, EQUALITY, POWER: A THEMATIC BRAID

For many white Americans in the 1840s, Manifest Destiny incorporated both liberty and power. Expansionists almost reflexively believed it their free right to occupy virtually all of North America. Regardless of belief, Americans knew they had the power to acquire the territory they coveted. The Anglo-Saxon version of civilization—the only version blessed by Providence, expansionists believed—must replace those of Native Americans, Mexicans, and even that of religious dissenters, such as the Mormons. The Democratic Party defined progress as spreading American institutions over space, while the Whigs defined it as improving institutions over time.

As territory was acquired, another question of power arose. In the lands obtained by annexation, treaty, or war, which settlement pattern would be used? Would the South's reliance on slavery spread to these new areas? Or would the North's commitment to free labor prevail? Even with slave states and free states at odds over a number of issues, the political implications of slavery's expansion became enormously important. That so many Americans, North and South, viewed this issue as one that permitted little room for compromise doomed to failure the Compromise of 1850 and also other attempts to create harmony within the Union.

For other American groups, liberty, equality, and power became enmeshed in the westward movement as well. Indians suffered a loss of territory, freedom of movement, and cultural strength as their lands came under federal control. Black Americans had much at stake in regard to slavery's possible expansion. For American women, the reluctance—and resistance—on the part of many women to move to the frontiers brought the realization that, in marriage and the family, patriarchy still ruled. They had little choice but to follow men to the new lands.

IDENTIFICATIONS

John Tyler	Santa Fe Trail
Manifest Destiny	Young America
Oregon fever	Lewis Cass
Santa Fe Trail	Oregon Trail
Joseph Smith	Mormon migration
Great American Desert	Conscience Whigs
Antonio Lopez de Santa Anna	Free Soil Party
Sam Houston	Compromise of 1850
"Fifty-four Forty or Fight!"	Daniel Webster
Winfield Scott	Stephen A. Douglas
Rio Grande	John C. Frémont
Battle of Buena Vista	Fugitive Slave Act of 1850
Treaty of Guadalupe Hidalgo	*Uncle Tom's Cabin*
Anthony Burns	Harriet Beecher Stowe
Wilmot Proviso	filibustering
Ostend Manifesto	William Walker
Liberty Party	

CHRONOLOGY

1836	Mexican army captures the Alamo.
	Texans defeat the Mexican army at San Jacinto.
1840	Richard Henry Dana publishes *Two Years before the Mast*.
1840s	"Young America" movement defines the nation's Manifest Destiny.
1842	*Prigg* v. *Pennsylvania* declares the state's antikidnapping law unconstitutional.
1842–1843	"Oregon fever" impels thousands to move to the Oregon Country.
1844	Anti-Mormon mob kills Joseph Smith in Illinois.
	James K. Polk elected president.
1845	United States annexes Texas.
1846	Mexican War begins.
	American settlers led by John C. Frémont capture Sonoma, California.
	Wilmot Proviso causes great controversy over slavery's expansion.
1847	Brigham Young leads the Mormons west to the Great Basin.
	Mexico City falls to the United States Army.
1848	Treaty of Guadalupe Hidalgo ends the Mexican War.
	Popular sovereignty proposed by Lewis Cass.
	Free Soil Party forms.
	Gold discovered in California.
	Zachary Taylor wins the presidency.
1849	California gold rush begins.
1850	Henry Clay and Stephen A. Douglas craft the Compromise.
	John C. Calhoun and Zachary Taylor die.
	Millard Fillmore sworn in as president.
	California admitted as a free state.
1851	Fugitive slaves laws enacted.
1852	*Uncle Tom's Cabin* is published.
1854	Ostend Manifesto causes uproar over Cuba.
	William Walker leads filibustering expedition to Nicaragua.

THEMATIC TOPICS FOR ENRICHMENT

1. Describe what Manifest Destiny meant for white laborers and farmers in the 1840s. What did it mean for slave owners?

2. Discuss what Manifest Destiny held in store for western Native Americans. What did Manifest Destiny mean for black Americans?

3. Discuss the various reasons Americans went west in the 1840s.

4. Why did Texans seek independence from Mexico in the 1830s? Why did they want the United States to annex Texas?

5. Discuss how California and the actions of President Taylor led to a sectional crisis at the end of 1849.

6. What were the provisions of the Fugitive Slave Act that upset northerners? Describe how northerners reacted to the act's enforcement.

GEOGRAPHY OBJECTIVES

1. On a map of the United States, identify the states carved out of Jefferson's Louisiana Purchase between 1803 and 1846 (p. 437).

2. Sketch the route of the Santa Fe Trail from Independence, Missouri, to Santa Fe, and the Oregon Trail from Independence to Portland, Oregon (p. 439).

3. Find the Oregon Territory on a map and contrast Polk's campaign pledge of 54′40″ with the ultimate treaty line of the forty-ninth parallel (p. 444).

4. On a map of the western United States, shade the territory acquired by the United States between the 1819 Adams-Onís Treaty and the Treaty of Guadalupe-Hidalgo thirty years later (p. 447).

SUGGESTED ESSAY TOPICS

1. Define the concept of Manifest Destiny and assess its impact upon American politics in the 1840s.

2. Assess the causes and consequence of the United States's war with Mexico. Why did many Americans oppose the war?

3. Contrast the platforms of the Liberty Party, the Free Soil party, and the Conscience Whigs. What views did all three share?

4. What issues did the Compromise of 1850 resolve? Which ones did it not?

LECTURE OUTLINE

1. Citizens of almost all regions of the country in the 1840s instinctively viewed **territorial growth** as the American way, as the country's right-of-way. Indians and Mexicans could not stop this juggernaut.
   a. Many northerners understood that **Manifest Destiny** and slavery were intimately tied together, as new lands in the South spelled the expansion of the "peculiar institution."

   (Show Transparency 13-02: Map, Free and Slave States and Territories, 1848)

   b. As old as the first seventeenth-century settlers, Americans' **westering impulse** proved as much a northern as a southern phenomenon.
   c. The **Oregon and California Trails** served as routes for literally hundreds of thousands to make their way, often at great peril, into the alluring lands of the West as "Oregon fever" swept the country.

   (Show Transparency 13-03: Map, Overland Trails, 1846)

   d. Joseph Smith gave his life in leading the remarkable **Mormon migration**, which culminated in Brigham Young's settlement of the Utah Territory in 1847.
   e. American expansionists, led by Sam Houston, founded the **Republic of Texas** in March of 1836.

    f. Texans' desire to join the United States precipitated the Annexation Controversy in Congress during the administration of **John Tyler**.

    g. Dark horse candidate **James Knox Polk** made the acquisition of Texas and Oregon the key planks of his successful campaign for the presidency in 1844.

    (Show Transparency 13-01: 1846 Anti-Polk Cartoon)

2. Deliberate American provocations resulted in a two-year land grab called the **Mexican War**.

    (Show Transparency 13-04: Map, Principal Campaigns of the Mexican War, 1846–1847)

    a. The military campaigns of 1846 proved highly successful, particularly in California, but created a formidable Whig presidential prospect in **Zachary Taylor**, "Old Rough and Ready," who led his forces to successive victories in Texas.

    b. The military campaigns of 1847 proved even more successful, with the rather meager army of **Winfield Scott** performing an amphibious landing at **Vera Cruz**, decimating a larger Mexican force and capturing Mexico City.

    c. Northerners, ever skeptical of southern motives, publicly and vociferously expressed their heart-felt **antiwar sentiment**.

    d. Reservations about war aims led the House to pass the **Wilmot Proviso**, which sought the exclusion of slavery from all territory acquired in the war.

3. The overlapping issues of territorial expansion and slavery dominated the politics of the **election of 1848** and promised to plague the short-lived presidency of Louisianan Zachary Taylor.

    a. Northern antislavery activists founded the **Free Soil Party** upon the same principals as those of the Wilmot Proviso.

    b. The year 1849 marked the start of the **gold rush** and the subsequent movement for **California statehood**.

4. While hailed by many as the savior of the Union, the **Compromise of 1850** in its final form only delayed the ultimate breakdown of the party system.

    a. The **Senate debates** over the 1850 Compromise revolved around the efforts of Clay and Webster, who supported compromise, and Calhoun, who opposed it.

    b. The **passage of the Compromise** as an omnibus bill proved impossible but succeeded under the clever direction of freshman Senator Stephen A. Douglas of Illinois.

    c. Northerners found anathema the **Fugitive Slave Law**, despite the stirring rhetoric of Daniel Webster.

    d. Southern representatives condemned **fugitive slave escapes**, such as that of Anthony Burns, while many antislavery advocates materially supported the Underground Railroad.

    e. No one event more contributed to antislavery sentiment than Harriet Beecher Stowe's ***Uncle Tom's Cabin***, published in 1852 and reprinted many times subsequently.

5. Southern expansionists sought through **filibustering** expeditions to acquire more lands for the expansion of slavery.

    i. Filibusters, like the supporters of the Ostend Manifesto, believed that Manifest Destiny included American slave colonies in the Caribbean and Central America.

ii. The most remarkable of the filibusteros was William Walker, the **gray-eyed man of destiny**, who after naming himself president of Nicaragua was later executed by a firing squad in Honduras while attempting another coup.

American Album: The California Gold Rush

Conclusion: Americans termed "Manifest Destiny" the notion that North America ought to be the sole domain of white Americans and their institutions. Manifest Destiny justified the acquisition through war and treachery of over 1.1 million square miles of territory at the end of the 1840s. While few disavowed the acquisition of new territory, many northerners suspected that expansion westward was a vehicle for the expansion of the South's peculiar institution.

TEACHING RESOURCES

Frederick Douglass: When the Lion Wrote History is a documentary on the "most influential black man" of the nineteenth century. PBS Video (90 minutes).

The Donner Party gives the tragic history of the ill-fated group trying to reach California in 1846. PBS Video (90 minutes).

The Oregon Trail is a four-part documentary of the 1840s land rush to Oregon. Films for the Humanities & Sciences (25 minutes each, color).

"The Golden Land," in *The West of the Imagination* series, documents the West in the 1830s and 1840s. Films for the Humanities & Sciences (52 minutes, color).

Texas and the Mexican Cession is the history of Texas's quest for independence. Filmic Archives (14 minutes).

Gold Rush and the Settlement of California provides an account of the developments in 1848–1849 in the West. Filmic Archives (16 minutes).

The West, episodes two and three, discusses the American westward expansion often called Manifest Destiny. PBS Video (60 minutes each).

Chapter 14
The Gathering Tempest, 1853–1860

CHAPTER SUMMARY

Within five years after passage of the Compromise of 1850, the fragile peace between the North and South shattered. The controversy over the Fugitive Slave Act and the reaction to *Uncle Tom's Cabin* contributed to the collapse of sectional harmony. But even more important were the demise of the Whig Party and the reemergence of the slavery expansion issue, particularly in the Kansas Territory.

Northern and southern Whigs had divided over the California question and what southern Whigs saw as Zachary Taylor's betrayal. By 1852, many had joined the southern Democrats and helped to elect the Democratic presidential candidate, Franklin Pierce. Further dividing the party was a new wave of nativism that drew many Whigs into the American party—better known as the Know Nothings—which focused on anti-Catholic and anti-immigrant issues rather than those on which the Whig Party had been founded.

The Kansas-Nebraska Act destroyed what peace had been gained with the Compromise of 1850. Stephen A. Douglas's collaboration with David Atchinson and other proslavery leaders to organize the two territories on the basis of popular sovereignty—with the tacit understanding that Kansas would develop as a slave territory—infuriated northerners and reawakened fears of the "Slave Power" of the South. As a result of northern anger over the act's passage, northern Democrats lost much support, and the Republican Party emerged to replace the Whigs in a new two-party system. By 1856, the Republicans had constructed a sectional but powerful organization that was dedicated to wresting national power from the Democrats and preventing the spread of slavery to any new territory.

The settlement of Kansas in 1854 and 1855 proved that popular sovereignty was unworkable. Free-soil battled proslavery settlers, the latter aided by "border ruffians" from neighboring Missouri. By 1856, Kansas had both a proslavery territorial government and a free-soil government, with each claiming to be legitimate. When proslavery forces sacked Lawrence and John Brown attacked Pottawatomie Creek, America referred to the area as "Bleeding Kansas."

The issue of Kansas divided the Democratic Party along sectional lines. President James Buchanan's ill-advised support of the proslavery faction in the territory and its Lecompton constitution forced Stephen Douglas to admit that the proslavery side (through election fraud and intimidation) had made a mockery of popular sovereignty. Douglas's insistence that fair elections be held in Kansas cost him southern Democratic support and virtually doomed his presidential hopes.

The sectional division deepened with the Dred Scott Supreme Court decision and the Panic of 1857. In the Scott case, the southern-dominated Court blasted both the free-soil and popular-sovereignty positions on slavery's expansion—only to discover that such an emotional issue as slavery's future in the territories could not be settled by a court ruling. Because the economic recession of 1857 seemed to affect the North more than the South, southern leaders could not resist touting their own slave-based economy as being superior to that of the free labor system in the North.

According to George Fitzhugh and other southern apologists, the slave was better off and happier than the free worker in the North. Despite enormous northern economic expansion in the 1850s, James Hammond and other southern leaders proclaimed that "cotton is king."

The decade ended with violent reaction to John Brown's raid on Harpers Ferry. Brown's plans for a slave revolt reawakened the increasingly paranoid southerners' greatest fear. They perceived the North as being filled with John Browns ready to launch further bloody attacks on the South. Even more perilous to the Union, they viewed the Republican Party as the harborer and instigator of fanatics like Brown and vowed to leave the Union if Republicans won the presidency in 1860.

LIBERTY, EQUALITY, POWER: A THEMATIC BRAID

In the 1850s, Kansas became the prize in the quest for more political power by both the North and the South. More votes in Congress meant more control over the national agenda and the nation's future. But even more for the proslavery side, Kansas, if it became a slave territory, meant the end to the northern blockade on slavery's expansion. Some southern leaders, such as David Atchinson, perceived Kansas as the first of many territories where slavery could be established successfully. So important was Kansas to the free-soil and proslavery camps that hundreds of families moved to Kansas to cast ballots for their particular stand on the slavery issue, and both sides were prepared to resort to violence if balloting failed to produce the desired results. More determined yet were proslavery Missourians who used force to win Kansas for their side.

The slavery expansion issue involved such a struggle for power that traditional ways of settling disputes over power—the ballot and the courts—worked less and less well as the decade continued. Neither side accepted the outcome of the Kansas elections. Southerners threatened to leave the Union if voters ever put Republicans into power in the national government. By its ruling in the Dred Scott case, the Supreme Court found that much of the nation could not have cared less about what the courts had to say about slavery's expansion.

Meanwhile, definitions of liberty and equality were the subject of much debate. As Abraham Lincoln asked, were all men created equal, or did this truth apply only to white men? Or to Protestants and not Catholics? Or did equality apply just to native-born citizens and not immigrants? Ultimately, the question became whether the United States was the champion of herrenvolk democracy—democracy for the master race—or the champion for a political system that embraced whites and the other races, native-born and immigrant, men and women, Protestant and Catholic.

The depth of the sectional division over freedom was revealed when John C. Calhoun and other southerners proclaimed that slavery protected the freedom of all whites by uniting all classes of whites to ensure that slavery of the black race continued. For Lincoln and many of his northern contemporaries, this could not be more wrong. Either slavery or freedom would have to die.

IDENTIFICATIONS

David R. Atchinson	Stephen A. Douglas
Abraham Lincoln	American System of Manufactures
McCormick Reaper	*DeBow's Review*
Kansas-Nebraska Act	John C. Frémont
Republican Party	*The Impending Crisis of the South*
King Cotton	Hinton Rowan Helper
Know-Nothings	Panic of 1857
nativism	Wendell Phillips
Archbishop John Hughes	herrenvolk democracy

Bleeding Kansas
Lecompton Constitution
Charles Sumner
"Crime Against Kansas" Speech
Roger B. Taney
Freeport Question
John Brown
Pottawatomie Creek
James Hammond

"border ruffians"
George Fitzhugh
Preston Brooks
Dred Scott
Lincoln-Douglas debates
"Wide Awake" clubs
Harpers Ferry
James Buchanan
ideology

CHRONOLOGY

1846	*DeBow's Review* first published in New Orleans.
1851	Crystal Palace exhibit in London draws great attention.
1852	The American (Know-Nothing) Party becomes significant political factor.
1854	Congress passes the Kansas-Nebraska Act.
	Republican Party forms in Wisconsin.
	"Know-Nothings" gain strength on nativist agenda.
1854–1856	Crimean War rocks Europe.
1855	"Bleeding Kansas" develops as free-soil settlers refuse to accept proslavery election fraud.
1856	Lawrence, Kansas, sacked by proslavery mob.
	John Brown murders proslavery defenders at Pottawatomie Creek.
	Preston Brooks canes Charles Sumner in Senate chamber.
	James Buchanan defeats Republican John C. Frémont and nativist Millard Fillmore for the presidency.
1857	Dred Scott decision rendered by the Supreme Court.
	Economic recession begins with the Panic.
	George Fitzhugh publishes *Cannibals All*.
	Hinton R. Helper issues *The Impending Crisis of the South*.
	Lecompton Constitution written by Kansas proslavery forces.
1858	Lincoln delivers his House Divided speech.
	Great Debates between Illinoisans Lincoln and Douglas foreshadow upcoming presidential race.
1859	John Brown raids Harpers Ferry; Brown hanged after conviction.

THEMATIC TOPICS FOR ENRICHMENT

1. Discuss the motivations in 1854 for repealing the Missouri Compromise and organizing Kansas and Nebraska on the basis of popular sovereignty.

2. What was the "black belt," and why was it so named?.

3. Why did "nativism" reemerge in the 1850s in the form of the "Know-Nothing" political movement? Who were the nativists' targets? Why?

4. Why did Kansas become "Bleeding Kansas" in the mid-1850s? Explain why Missourians believed that they had to interfere in Kansas politics.

5. Discuss the issues behind the Dred Scott decision. Why did the Court rule the way it did? Why did many ignore its ruling?

6. Explain why the national economy expanded so greatly in the 1850s and how this expansion played a role in sectional politics.

7. Contrast George Fitzhugh's concept of slavery with that of Hinton R. Helper.

8. Compare the northern reaction to John Brown in 1859 with the southern reaction.

9. What were the differences between "free-labor ideology" and the southern version of herrenvolk democracy?

GEOGRAPHY OBJECTIVES

1. Locate Kansas and Nebraska on a map. Which states abut Kansas (p. 475)?

2. Compare the transportation systems of the North and South in the 1850s (p. 482).

3. Outline the region named the "black belt" and identify which states it lies within (p. 487).

SUGGESTED ESSAY TOPICS

1. What was Stephen Douglas's rationale for the 1854 Kansas-Nebraska Act? Why did the passages of the act lead to "Bleeding Kansas" and so much discord in American politics?

2. What was the "free labor" ideology of the Republican Party?

3. Explain the Dred Scott case, Taney's decision, and their impact on sectional strife.

4. Contrast the economies of the North and South. Why had they diverged so greatly in the preceding three decades?

LECTURE OUTLINE

1. Nothing contributed more to the sense of sectional crisis than the fight over slavery in **Kansas**. The rise of the **Republican Party** in opposition to the spread of slavery and to slaveholders' interests anywhere guaranteed that slavery would dominate the political debates of the remainder of the 1850s.
   a. The brainchild of Stephan A. Douglas of Illinois, the **Kansas-Nebraska Act** of 1854 repealed the Missouri Compromise line that had marked the northern border of slave expansion in the Louisiana Purchase.
   b. The sectional fighting over slavery and related issues led directly to the **death of the Whig Party**, as northern Whigs joined the Republican Party.

2. Concerns over immigration and **nativism** proved important political issues that in other times might have overshadowed the growing crisis over slavery.
   a. A visceral fear of **immigrants in politics** among many Protestants resulted in the formation of the American, or Know-Nothing, Party.

b. The rise of the **"Know-Nothings"** culminated in the candidacy of Millard Fillmore for president in 1856 on a platform of immigrant restriction and delay of full political rights to newcomers.

c. The furor over slavery was coterminous with the **decline of nativism**, itself critical to any chance of Republican success in national politics.

3. A virtual civil war known as **Bleeding Kansas** broke out in that territory, as competing pro- and antislavery factions battled for supremacy.

(Show Transparency 14-02: Map, Kansas-Nebraska and the Slavery Issue)

a. Charles Sumner's **"Crime against Kansas"** speech so inflamed South Carolina Representative Preston Brooks that he nearly beat Sumner to death. Brooks's caning of the Massachusetts senator was as hailed in the South as it was condemned in the North.

(Show Transparency 14-01: Congressman Preston Brooks beating Senator Charles Sumner)

4. The Republican's first presidential candidate, John C. Frémont, ran well in the **election of 1856** but failed to win enough Border States to defeat Democrat James Buchanan.

a. In the **Dred Scott Case**, Supreme Court Chief Justice Roger B. Taney ruled that the Missouri Compromise constituted an illegal denial of the property rights of slaveholders and that slaves were not citizens and, therefore, could not sue in court.

b. President Buchanan endorsed Kansas's blatantly proslavery **Lecompton Constitution**, despite the vehement opposition of Stephen Douglas and other northern Democrats.

5. The **economy in the 1850s** hummed along as economic production even outstripped the prodigious rate of population increase.

(Show Transparency 14-03: Map, Main Transportation Routes in the 1850s)

a. Contemporaries heaped praise on "Yankee ingenuity" and the so-called **"American system of manufactures,"** which incorporated the wide-scale use of interchangeable parts and other technical innovations.

b. The **southern economy** grew rapidly in the 1850s, largely on the basis of growing worldwide demand for cotton.

c. The inherent dangers of the **sovereignty of king cotton** were noted by James D. B. De Bow and other southerners who favored diversification and modernization of techniques.

(Show Transparency 14-04: Map, Slavery and Staple Crops in the South, 1860)

d. While northern leaders espoused the glories of free labor, **labor conditions in the North** were often miserable, as wages were low and urban life unhealthy in the extreme.

e. While the **Panic of 1857** hit hardest in the industrial areas of the North, the Republican Party actually gained strength due to southern opposition to economic reform bills.

    f. **Sectionalism and the Panic** went hand in hand, as northern interests exploited southern politicians' intransigence on economic reform measures.

    g. The **free labor ideology** of "free soil, free labor, free men" was at the heart of the Republican Party's sectional message in the 1850s.

    h. Republicans skillfully exploited the publication of North Carolinian Hinton Rowan Helper's *The Impending Crisis* to demonstrate how slavery negatively affected the material conditions of non-slaveholders.

    i. While few **southern non-slaveholders** seemed to be aware of the negative impact of slavery on their economic fortunes, most understood that their white skin made them part of the "ruling race" of their region.

6. The **Lincoln-Douglas debates** of 1858 served to highlight the deep divide over the morality of slavery in Illinois, and the North generally, and quickly came to be regarded as perhaps the finest example of stump speech eloquence from the era.

    a. Abraham Lincoln stirred great controversy when, upon accepting the Senate nomination, he declared that the Union could not forever remain "a house divided."

    b. Douglas lost any chance of southern extremist support for his 1860 presidential campaign when he espoused in his **"Freeport doctrine"** that citizens could effectively exclude slavery from the territories.

7. The capture of abolitionist **John Brown at Harpers Ferry** and his subsequent execution stirred the conscience of northerners who previously had considered abolitionists to be nothing less than dangerous disunionists.

American Album: The Lincoln-Douglas Debates

Conclusion: Despite the efforts of many politicians, who feared for the Union, the events of the 1850s reinforced the growing schism between slavery and freedom. The birth of the Republican Party and the election of Lincoln inexorably led southerners to reconsider the value of remaining within the United States, while John Brown's raid at Harpers Ferry proved true the South's greatest fears.

TEACHING RESOURCES

America Grows Up (1850–1900s) offers an overview of the nation's economic development. Filmic Archives (53 minutes).

On a Clear Day You Can See Boston describes the Irish immigration to the nation in the 1850s. Films for the Humanities & Sciences (52 minutes, color).

Go West, Young Man covers the Norwegian movement to the Midwest. Films for the Humanities & Sciences (52 minutes, color).

Out of Ireland focuses on Irish immigrants who arrived in the mid–nineteenth century. PBS Video (111 minutes).

Lincoln: Making of a President describes his formative years and his rise to national prominence during the Lincoln–Douglas debates. Movies Unlimited (60 minutes).

The Civil War: Union at Risk presents the prewar differences between North and South and emphasizes Constitutional interpretation. Filmic Archives (25 minutes, color).

Chapter 15
Secession and Civil War, 1860–1862

CHAPTER SUMMARY

The 1860 election completed the split between the North and the South. Unable to decide between popular sovereignty and proslavery platforms, the Democratic Party split into northern and southern fragments, ending the South's last political tie to the North. Southern Democrats chose John C. Breckinridge as their presidential candidate; northern Democrats picked Stephen A. Douglas. The Constitutional Union Party, mainly a collection of border-state former Whigs, opted to run Tennessean John Bell for the presidency. The Republicans, needing only to unite the North for victory, nominated Abraham Lincoln. After a lively campaign in which the Republicans broadened their appeal by adding economic issues to their platform and the southern Democrats vowed to leave the Union if they lost the election, the upstart Republican Party, just six years old, won virtually every northern state and with them the presidency.

Secession fever ran rampant in the South. Believing that secession was a constitutional right—simply the reverse of the decision to join the Union—South Carolina and six other Deep South states "withdrew" from the United States by February of 1861. Northerners argued that the decision to join the Union was irreversible, that the "doctrine of secession is anarchy." They bitterly opposed southerners on this constitutional issue. Efforts to reach a compromise in this national crisis, however, failed. Only the Crittenden proposal to guarantee slavery and to extend it into the territories drew much interest, and it was rejected by both the Republicans and the secessionists.

In the beginning of February in Montgomery, Alabama, delegates from the seceded states created the Confederate States of America and called for the other eight slave states to join their new nation. For their constitution, they simply copied, word for word, much of the U.S. Constitution, changing it, primarily, only to give more power to the states and additional explicit protection to slavery. With the exception of a few military installations, such as Fort Sumter and Fort Pickins, the Confederates seized federal property and expelled U.S. officials from Confederate soil.

Lincoln's hopes to buy time to allow southern unionism to reassert itself collapsed with the Fort Sumter situation. Offering only humanitarian assistance to the fort's soldiers, the new president brilliantly turned Fort Sumter into a Confederate dilemma. In the predawn hours of April 12, the Confederates attacked the fort; thirty hours later Fort Sumter capitulated. The Civil War had begun. Lincoln asked the states for 75,000 volunteers to put down the rebellion.

For the border states especially, the time to choose sides had arrived. Virginia, North Carolina, Arkansas, and Tennessee went with the Confederacy. Missouri, Kentucky, Maryland, and Delaware chose to stay in the Union. In many of the border states, strong dissent on the secession issue resulted in isolated incidents of guerrilla warfare, creating wars within the Civil War.

The Union had enormous advantages over the Confederacy. In manpower, industrial output, banking resources, trade, and transportation, the North stood supreme over the South. But for a decisive victory, Union forces would have to conquer and occupy much of the South, whereas Confederate forces only would have to stop the northern invasions and bide their time until the northerners became tired of war and went home.

Neither side believed that the war would last very long or had any idea of just how bloody the conflict would be. The rifle, with its "Minié ball" bullets, took a terrible toll on both sides and forced changes in tactics. Steam-powered, armor-plated naval ships, naval mines, and other innovations changed battle on the seas. Railroads and telegraphs forced generals to adopt new strategies to match these technological advances.

The war's financing brought runaway inflation and economic misery to the South. Unable or unwilling to tax or borrow enough money, the Confederate government issued paper money, which rapidly became worthless. Also a failure was the South's King Cotton policy, which denied the Confederacy money from the production of cotton, its chief asset, and still did not force Great Britain and other European nations to give the Confederacy diplomatic recognition. The Union navy's blockade of southern shipping became more effective after 1862, and, with internal transportation problems within the Confederacy, food shortages afflicted a growing number of Confederate citizens.

Bull Run, the first major battle of the Civil War, elated southerners and stunned northerners as it turned into a Union debacle. Even after George McClellan regrouped northern forces and turned them into the formidable Army of the Potomac, Union fortunes in the Virginia theater did not improve greatly. McClellan's 1862 "peninsula campaign" failed to take Richmond, the Confederate capital. John Pope and his Union army failed to stop Robert E. Lee and his Army of Northern Virginia at the second battle of Bull Run and left Maryland open to Lee's invasion.

West of the Appalachians, the Union fared better. In February 1862, Ulysses S. Grant's forces took control of the Tennessee and Cumberland Rivers by taking Forts Henry and Donelson. Nashville became the first Confederate state capital to fall to Union forces. After a setback on the first day of the battle of Shiloh, Grant regrouped, won the battle, and forced the Confederates into northern Mississippi. Meanwhile, Union ships under David Farragut's command took control of the mouth of the Mississippi and forced New Orleans to capitulate. By the summer of 1862, only at Port Hudson and Vicksburg did the Confederacy have control of the Mississippi.

LIBERTY, EQUALITY, POWER: A THEMATIC BRAID

The power struggle between North and South evolved from political in 1860 to military in 1861. Determined to force northern Democrats to support slavery's expansion by threatening to destroy the party, Deep South delegates at the Democratic conventions in 1860 bolted, snapping the Democratic tie between the two sections. Facing two Democratic presidential candidates and one from the Constitutional Union Party, Republicans were able to gain power merely by uniting the North. Lincoln was swept into the presidency, and northern strength in Congress increased.

For southern leaders, this was an unacceptable shift in political fortunes. Since 1789, the president, the House Speaker, and the president pro tem of the Senate had been southerners two thirds of the time. The Supreme Court, too, had been a southern power base. This enormous influence in the direction of the nation's course had eroded to the point that many southerners feared that the "southern way" had been contained by the Republican surge and that they faced an uncertain future even within the South. The question for many southerners after Lincoln's victory was whether it was wise to stay in a Union that no longer protected southern interests or to secede and create their own union of slave states.

Did they have the right to secede? Southerners argued that secession was an option because states still retained their sovereignty after they had joined the Union. They now wished to reclaim this power to control their own affairs. Northerners vehemently disagreed. The Union was not a collection of sovereign states but an indivisible political entity. If one minority left the majority, other minorities would follow until the Union would be, as James Buchanan put it, a "rope of sand." As the war soon proved, secession was not a right, but a question of power—military power.

IDENTIFICATIONS

John C. Breckinridge	Constitutional Union Party
fire-eaters	Crittenden Compromise
Confederate States of America	John Bell
Jefferson Davis	Alexander H. Stephens
Fort Sumter	George B. McClellan
Major Robert Anderson	Robert E. Lee
Wilson's Creek Battle	David Farragut
First Manassas (Bull Run)	Army of the Potomac
William H. Seward	Forts Henry and Donelson
Ulysses S. Grant	battle of Shiloh
West Virginia	Thomas J. (Stonewall) Jackson
Minié ball	Army of Northern Virginia
Vicksburg	Shenandoah Valley
King Cotton diplomacy	Army of Tennessee
greenbacks	Seven Days' Battle
blockade runners	second battle of Bull Run
Trent affair	Nathan Bedford Forrest
The *Monitor* and the *Virginia*	Anaconda Plan

CHRONOLOGY

1858	William Seward delivers his "Irrepressible Conflict" speech.
1860	Democratic Party splits.
	Lincoln elected president.
	South Carolina secedes.
	United States Army occupies Fort Sumter.
1861	Crittenden Compromise fails to keep the Union together.
	Kansas becomes the thirty-fourth state.
	Ten states eventually join South Carolina to create the Confederate States of America.
	Jefferson Davis named president of the Confederacy.
	Fort Sumter falls and the Civil War begins.
	Tennessee, Virginia, North Carolina, and Arkansas join the Confederacy.
	Union Navy blockades southern ports.
	Trent affair almost causes war between United States and Great Britain.
	Battle of Bull Run (July 21).
	George McClellan assumes command of the Army of the Potomac.
1862	Ulysses S. Grant's forces take Forts Henry and Donelson (February 6 and February 16).
	Battle of the *Virginia* and the *Monitor* marks a major change in naval warfare.
	Battle of Shiloh (April 6–7).
	Union Navy captures New Orleans.

McClellan's peninsula campaign ends with the Seven Days' battles.

Robert E. Lee assumes command of the Army of Northern Virginia.

Second battle of Bull Run (August 29–30).

1863   West Virginia becomes the thirty-fifth state.

THEMATIC TOPICS FOR ENRICHMENT

1. What economic stands did the Republicans take in 1860 that attracted northern voters?

2. Give the details of the Crittenden Compromise and explain why both Lincoln and the secessionists rejected the Compromise.

3. In what ways did the Confederate Constitution differ from the United States Constitution?

4. Discuss how Fort Sumter developed into a dilemma for both the Union and the Confederacy.

5. Discuss how each side in the Civil War attempted to finance its participation in the conflict. Why did the Confederacy fail in this regard?

6. Discuss military innovations in the Civil War and how they affected how battles were fought and wars were planned.

7. Explain why Union fortunes were better in western areas in 1862 than they were in the Virginia theater.

GEOGRAPHY OBJECTIVES

1. Assess the sectional character of the 1860 presidential election on a map of the United States (p. 507).

2. Locate the slave states that remained within the Union during the Civil War (p. 507).

3. Identify the states in which the majority of the battles of the Civil War were fought (p. 515).

4. Assess the importance of railroads and rivers in the fighting of the Civil War (p. 515).

SUGGESTED ESSAY TOPICS

1. Why did both national political parties, the Whigs and the Democrats, ultimately split up on the years leading up to the Civil War?

2. Considering that Lincoln explicitly stated that he was not an abolitionist, why did South Carolina secede from the Union upon his election in 1860?

3. Assess the great difficulty in choosing sides as the Civil War broke out in 1861, particularly for residents of the border states.

4. Contrast Union and Confederate relative advantages in preparing to fight a protracted civil war. What did the Union have to do to win the war? What did the Confederacy need to do to gain its independence?

LECTURE OUTLINE

1. Although Lincoln won a clear electoral majority, the **election of 1860** was in many ways extraordinary; four candidates, Lincoln and Douglas of Illinois, Breckinridge of Kentucky, and Bell of Tennessee, representing three parties, vied for the presidency in what amounted to two separate elections.

   (Show Transparency 15-01: 1860 Election Cartoon)

   a. Disaffection with the perceived radicalism of the major candidates led the Republicans to nominate **Abraham Lincoln**, the favorite son of the Chicago convention.
   b. The nomination of Lincoln and the republican platform did nothing to quell **southern fears** of the dangers posed by a Republican victory in the upcoming election.

2. Following the Electoral College's confirmation of Lincoln's victory, South Carolina led the **Lower South's secession** from the Union.

   (Show Transparency 15-02: Map, Election of 1860 and Southern Secession)

   a. **Northerners affirmed the Union** by publicly supporting Lincoln and declaring secession unconstitutional.
   b. Northerners and southerners floated a number of compromise proposals, most notably that of **John J. Crittenden** of Kentucky, in a desperate effort to avert war in the first months of 1861.

3. Establishment of the **Confederacy** fell to a convention of seceded states that met in Montgomery, Alabama, in the beginning of February.

4. Lincoln brilliantly forced the hand of the Confederacy into firing the first shot of the Civil War at **Fort Sumter** on the morning of April 12, 1861.

5. For both states and individuals, **choosing sides** proved an agonizing dilemma with far-ranging consequences.

   (Show Transparency 15-03: Map, Principal Military Campaigns of the Civil War)

   a. In the aftermath of the firing on Fort Sumter, the **border states** were forced to choose sides, with Delaware, Kentucky, and Missouri choosing to remain in the Union.
   b. The Unionist western counties of Virginia seceded from their state in the creation of **West Virginia**.

6. From men to money to material, the **balance sheet of war** seemed to favor the Union.
   a. The Union's material advantages would not guarantee victory without **strategy and morale** equal to the daunting task at hand.
   b. The prodigious numbers of volunteers on both sides made initial **mobilization for war** far less difficult than after the fighting had started in earnest.
   c. The bloody engagements of the first years of the Civil War led to a revolution in the **weapons and tactics,** particularly as increasingly lethal weapons necessitated new battlefield tactics.
   d. Many contemporaries called the Civil War the first "modern war" because of the

incredibly complicated **logistics** involved in amassing, transporting, feeding, arming, and supplying the forces that fought on both sides.

    e. **Financing the war** proved a struggle for both sides, with the North relying on printing paper money and the scheming manipulations of financiers like Jay Cooke, and the Confederacy on anything and everything.

7. The Civil War was not fought exclusively on land but with **navies and blockades and through foreign relations**, all of which ultimately proved advantageous for the Union.

    a. The Confederacy mistakenly believed that **King Cotton diplomacy** would be its trump card, forcing the English into recognition of the Confederate States of America.

    b. In the **Trent Affair** of October 1861, the Union almost so gravely insulted the English so as to lead them into assisting the Confederacy.

    c. The **Confederate Navy** was composed largely of two purchased British vessels, the Alabama and the Florida, which captured or sank over 250 Union merchant vessels.

    d. The *Monitor* and *Virginia*, both ironclads, dueled to a draw in their famed March 9, 1862, encounter.

8. The campaigns and battles of 1861–1862 proved that the war would not end quickly, and that only great bloodshed and loss of life would bring the conflict to a conclusion. Battles such as **Shiloh** and **Antietam** cost both sides huge losses of men.

    a. With all the appearances of a smashing Union victory, the **battle of Bull Run** on July 21, 1861, turned into a Confederate triumph when Thomas Jackson's Virginia brigade held its line and General Johnston arrived from the Shenandoah Valley with reinforcements.

(Show Transparency 15-04: Map, Battle of Bull Run [Manassas], July 21, 1861)

    b. Union **Naval Operations** resulted in a series of victories over Confederate coastal fortifications and the forced surrender of New Orleans at the hands of Admiral David G. Farragut.

    c. Led by Ulysses S. Grant, combined Union forces won key victories at **Fort Henry and Fort Donelson** on the Tennessee and Cumberland rivers.

(Show Transparency 15-05: Map, Kentucky-Tennessee Theater, Winter-Spring 1862)

    d. Despite losses of some 13,000 men in two days of bloody fighting, the Union and Grant defeated Confederate forces at the **battle of Shiloh** on April 6–7.

(Show Transparency 15-06: Map, Battle of Shiloh, April 6–7, 1862)

    e. The Union's fortunes reversed dramatically in the spring of 1862 in the **Virginia theater**, as Johnston's army put McClellan's Army of the Potomac on the defensive and Jackson's "foot cavalry" wreaked havoc in the Shenandoah Valley.

    f. In the **Seven Days' battles** at the end of June 1862, Robert E. Lee's Army of Northern Virginia turned the momentum of the war in favor of the Confederacy by driving McClellan's larger force from the outskirts of Richmond back towards the James River.

(Show Transparency 15-07: Maps, Peninsula Campaign, April–May 1862 & Seven Days' Battles, June 25–July 1, 1862)

9. For the remainder of 1862, **Confederate counteroffensives** were designed to break the Union's will to fight, and at the **second battle of Bull Run**, the Confederates again demonstrated that Union victory, if it ever were to come, was a far way off.

(Show Transparency 15-08: Map, Second Battle of Manassas [Bull Run], August 29–30, 1862)

American Album: Confederate Dead on the Battlefield

Conclusion: The election of Lincoln and the subsequent secession of eleven southern states culminated in Civil War. Neither Lincoln nor any party—North or South—could have predicted in 1860 that within two years the country would be mired in a brutal war without any foreseeable end. Perhaps only a few abolitionists sensed that the war would spell the end of slavery in the United States.

TEACHING RESOURCES

The Civil War—episodes one, two, and three—by Ken Burns offers an award-winning account of the war's beginning and its first two years. PBS Video (99 minutes, 69 minutes, and 76 minutes, respectively).

The Divided Union: The American Civil War is a five-part history of the conflict. Filmic Archives (55 minutes each).

Civil War Journal, Volume I offers a thirteen-episode history of the war from a more personal point of view. Filmic Archives (650 minutes).

Ironclads: The Monitor and the Merrimac covers a turning point in naval history. Filmic Archives (30 minutes).

The Battle of Glorietta Pass: Gettysburg of the West recounts this battle in the West in 1862. Films for the Humanities & Sciences (28 minutes, black and white).

The Massachusetts 54th Colored Infantry illustrates the compelling story of African Americans' devotion to the Union as well as remarkable heroism. PBS Video (60 minutes).

Chapter 16
A New Birth of Freedom, 1862–1865

CHAPTER SUMMARY

When Confederate armies invaded Kentucky and Maryland in the late summer of 1862, northern hopes for a quick end to the war and the restoration of the Union ended. President Lincoln realized that a total war, where the Union would mobilize every resource at its disposal to crush the Confederacy, was the only option he could pursue. Total war meant, however, that the Union would have to deal with the issue of the abolition of slavery.

In the beginning of the war, Union soldiers fought only to restore the 1860 union of states. Any attempt to have made slavery's demise a war goal would have alienated border states and infuriated those Union soldiers who held racist beliefs. As Union armies advanced into slave states, however, thousands of slaves fled their owners and sought sanctuary in army camps. Union commanders soon declared runaways from Confederate sympathizers "contrabands" and refused to return them to their masters. Congress approved of this practice as a war measure, in order to deny Confederates a vital source of labor. By March 1862, the Union forbade the return of any slave who crossed Union lines, even slaves belonging to Unionists.

By the summer of 1862, Lincoln made abolition of slavery the second Union war goal. Growing pressure from within his own party to do something about slavery and the North's desire to crush southern "traitors" forced Lincoln's decision. As commander in chief, Lincoln had the power to order the seizure of enemy property, of which slaves were an integral part. The president shrewdly couched his emancipation proclamation in military terms, designed either to end the war or to take from the South its laboring class. At his cabinet's request, Lincoln agreed to issue his proclamation only after a significant northern battlefield victory.

The Confederate invasion of Maryland culminated in the battle of Antietam (Sharpsburg) on September 17, 1862. The armies of Robert E. Lee and George McClellan fought to a bloody standoff, but Lee's retreat to Virginia gave Lincoln the "victory" that he needed. On September 22, the president issued his preliminary proclamation, stating that rebellious states had until January 1 to cease hostilities or, on that day, all slaves in areas still in rebellion would be freed. Because this was a military measure, slaves in Union states and in former Confederate territory now controlled by the Union forces would not be affected. Union armies suddenly became armies of liberation.

Military reverses plagued the Union from December 1862 through the spring of 1863. The new Union commander in Virginia, Ambrose Burnside, suffered defeat at the battle of Fredericksburg, and Ulysses S. Grant's attempts to take Vicksburg on the Mississippi River bogged down. Northern hopes revived briefly with a victory at Stones River (Murfreesboro) on January 2. But in May still another Union general, Joseph Hooker, had his army routed in Virginia by Robert E. Lee's Confederates at the battle of Chancellorsville.

Northern woes in the winter of 1863 brought increased desertion from Union armies, war weariness from the northern home front, and calls for peace at any price from northern Democrats, the "Copperheads." Meanwhile, in the Confederacy, growing economic problems led to food shortages by the spring of 1863, culminating in bread riots in Richmond in April.

Tensions were exacerbated on both sides of the conflict when northern and southern governments passed conscription laws. Tension among the classes arose in the Confederacy when it allowed wealthy southerners to avoid the draft by hiring substitutes. Slaveowners or overseers were also exempted if their plantations had twenty or more slaves. The Union draft law of 1863 provided for substitutes as well, angering northerners unable to afford to avoid the draft. Northern resentment of the draft was based not only on racist fears but on economic fears as well. It was felt that working-class men were being drafted in order to free blacks from slavery, who would then move north to take white laborers' jobs. Racism of this kind led to the New York City draft riots in July 1863, in which huge mobs destroyed draft offices, looted homes, and lynched several blacks.

The Civil War did not leave the roles of American women untouched. While a few on both sides served as spies or, by disguising themselves as men, as soldiers, most worked as clerks, secretaries, and nurses. Women volunteers also organized relief organizations, such as the Sanitary Commission. Women's wartime service spurred the nascent women's rights movement to drive for equality between the sexes.

The high tide of the Confederacy came with Lee's victory at Chancellorsville. Determined to demonstrate the Confederacy's power and perhaps to win recognition from abroad, Lee proposed an invasion of Pennsylvania and led his army northward to the battle of Gettysburg, the most important battle of the war. From July 1 through July 3, the battle raged between Lee's Army of Northern Virginia and George Meade's Army of the Potomac. On the third day, Lee launched a direct frontal assault on Union lines (Pickett's charge) only to suffer a devastating defeat. The Confederate army's retreat from Pennsylvania marked a turning point in the war. On July 4, Grant's Union forces took Vicksburg. Within a few days, Port Hudson fell as well, giving the Union complete control of the Mississippi River. Confederate fortunes revived briefly with a victory at the Battle of Chickamauga in September. Undaunted, Grant's army broke the siege of Chattanooga in November and routed the Confederates from Missionary Ridge.

Momentum shifted to the Union side, and was, in part, due to the efforts of black men fighting in the Union forces. African Americans felt that they were fighting for equal rights for their race. By 1863, the whites-only war ended, as the North enrolled free black men and emancipated slaves in the army and navy. Their officers remained white, but units such as the 54th Massachusetts Infantry proved their valor on the battlefield. Before the war ended, approximately 180,000 African-American males would serve the Union cause.

War weariness returned to the North in the spring and summer of 1864, and Lincoln entered the darkest hours of his presidency. With Grant as general in chief operating with the Army of the Potomac in Virginia, the Union advanced closer and closer to Richmond, but lost thousands of men in the battles of the Wilderness, Spotsylvania, and Cold Harbor. By autumn, Grant was bogged down in the siege of Petersburg, a railway center south of the Confederate capital. Meanwhile, William T. Sherman led a Union advance on Atlanta, but, by the end of July, seemed stalled before the city.

Democrats, hoping to oust Lincoln in the November election, once more called for peace at any price, even independence for the South, and nominated as their presidential candidate General George McClellan. Scrambling for support, the Republicans renamed their party the Union Party and chose a Democrat, Andrew Johnson of Tennessee, as Lincoln's vice presidential running mate. As the casualties mounted in the summer's battles, though, Lincoln gloomily predicted that he would not be reelected.

The president's woes disappeared rapidly in the fall of 1864. On September 2, Sherman's troops marched into Atlanta, and a few weeks later, Philip Sheridan's forces routed the Confederates out of Virginia's Shenandoah Valley. The Confederacy reeled toward collapse, and Lincoln swamped McClellan in the election.

In November and December, the Confederate plight worsened. The battles of Franklin and Nashville virtually destroyed the Army of Tennessee, the major Confederate force outside of Virginia, and Sherman's famed march across Georgia to Savannah broke the will of many southern people to continue to fight such a formidable enemy. By early 1865, Sherman's army launched a similar destructive march northward across South and North Carolina. In Virginia, relentless pressure on the Confederate forces caused them to abandon Petersburg and Richmond and retreat westward. On April 9 at Appomattox Courthouse, Robert E. Lee surrendered his army to Ulysses S. Grant, virtually ending the war. At the cost of four years of fighting and 625,000 lives lost, the nation had been preserved and slavery was abolished.

LIBERTY, EQUALITY, POWER: A THEMATIC BRAID

Lincoln's Emancipation Proclamation, even with its limits, effectively marked the end of slavery in America. The Thirteenth Amendment, when finally passed by Congress in January 1865 and ratified by the states in December of that same year, completed what Lincoln's proclamation and the Union forces had started.

The power to end slavery ultimately took the form of a constitutional amendment, but the real power to end slavery had come from the barrel of a gun. Not only did white Union soldiers make the end of slavery a war goal from 1862 onward, but the Union's enrollment of black soldiers and sailors permitted African Americans to fight for slavery's end as well. Their valiant service on the battlefields gave at least a temporary boost to the concept of racial equality.

American women, from both North and South, expanded their own roles during the war. Economically, the war opened new jobs for women in clerical work and nursing and forced many to assume the operation of farms, plantations, and businesses while men were away at war. Volunteer work to nurse the wounded and sick, to collect bandages and medicine for the armies, and to deliver books and other materials to soldiers drew the efforts of many more women. The dedicated and valuable service of women during the war gave hope to women's rights advocates that a grateful nation would reward them with equality of the sexes after the war.

IDENTIFICATIONS

Contrabands	Vicksburg
Copperheads	Chickamauga
battle of Antietam	54th Massachusetts Infantry
Emancipation Proclamation	Ulysses S. Grant
Ambrose E. Burnside	William T. Sherman
Joseph Hooker	Andersonville Prison
Clement L. Vallandigham	Philip Sheridan
bounty jumper	battle of Cedar Creek
Homestead Act	Fort Fisher
Morrill land-grant college act	Appomattox
Pacific Railroad Act	John Wilkes Booth
United States Sanitary Commission	Thirteenth Amendment
battle of Chancellorsville	battle of Gettysburg
Pickett's charge	Benjamin Butler
George McClellan	Fredericksburg
William S. Rosecrans	Richmond bread riot
New York City draft riots	Dr. Elizabeth Blackwell

Stonewall Jackson
George Thomas
Port Hudson
Wilderness
Cold Harbor
Horace Greeley
"march to the sea"

Joseph Johnston
Braxton Bragg
Fort Wagner
Spotsylvania
John Bell Hood
Fort Pillow

CHRONOLOGY

1862	Confederacy enacts conscription (April 16).
	Battle of Antietam (September 17).
	Lincoln issues the preliminary Emancipation Proclamation (September 22).
	Battle of Fredericksburg (December 13).
	Homestead Act and Morrill Act pass.
	Battle of Stones River (December 31–January 2).
1863	Lincoln signs the final Emancipation Proclamation (January 1).
	Union enacts conscription (March 3).
	Food riots break out in the Confederacy (April).
	Battle of Chancellorsville (May 1–5).
	Battle of Gettysburg (July 1–3).
	Vicksburg falls to Grant's besieging army (July 4).
	Port Hudson surrenders (July 9).
	Draft riots erupt in New York City (July 13–16).
	Battle of Chickamauga (September 19–20).
	Battle of Chattanooga (November 24–25).
1864	Grant becomes the Union's general in chief.
	Battle of the Wilderness (May 5–6).
	Battle of Spotsylvania (May 8–19).
	Siege of Petersburg begins (June).
	Atlanta falls to William T. Sherman's army (September 2).
	Philip Sheridan's forces rout Confederates from the Shenandoah Valley (October).
	Lincoln wins reelection (November).
	Sherman begins his march to the sea.
	Battles of Franklin (November 30) and Nashville (December 15–16) cripple the Confederates.
1865	Lee surrenders to Grant at Appomattox (April 9).
	Lincoln is assassinated (April 14).
	Last Confederate army surrenders (June 23).
	Thirteenth Amendment is ratified (December).

THEMATIC TOPICS FOR ENRICHMENT

1. Explain the writ of *habeas corpus* and why the Lincoln administration suspended it on occasion during the war.

2. Discuss the Clement L. Vallandigham affair and how it became an issue of treason versus freedom of speech.

3. Why are the battle of Gettysburg and the fall of Vicksburg often considered the turning point of the Civil War?

4. Discuss how black men became involved in the Union war effort and how they fared.

5. Describe how each side handled prisoners of war and how treatment of prisoners became a major controversy.

6. Why did General Sherman march across Georgia, and what were the results of his campaign?

GEOGRAPHY OBJECTIVES

1. Discuss the errors made by both Confederate and Union commanders at the battle of Antietam. Why was this battle, essentially a draw, still of extreme importance (p. 547)?

2. Illustrate Hooker's plans in 1863. Then explain how Robert E. Lee and Stonewall Jackson combined to foil those plans. (p. 557).

3. Identify the following locations, and note what occurred therein and/or thereby: Cemetery Hill, the Angle, Little Round Top, Devil's Den, Pickett's charge (p. 558).

4. Illustrate three different ways in which Ulysses S. Grant attempted to take Vicksburg. Use it further to explain fully why the final attempt in the summer of 1863 proved successful where the others had failed (p. 560).

5. Trace the course of the war in Tennessee and northern Georgia from the battle of Stones River through Union victory at Missionary Ridge (p. 561).

6. Illustrate Grant's strategy in the Wilderness campaign. Explain his major errors. Note also ways in which Grant's campaign differed from the earlier ones of Hooker, Burnside, or even McClellan (p. 566).

7. In what ways does the map on page 569 help explain why Jefferson Davis replaced Joseph Johnston with John Bell Hood? In what ways do the inset maps on the same page indicate that this may have been a mistake?

8. Trace the path of Hood's forces from Atlanta to Nashville. What was the purpose of this campaign? Why did it fail (p. 575)?

SUGGESTED ESSAY TOPICS

1. Trace the course of the military campaign in the Eastern Theater from Antietam to Appomattox, noting key battles and Union command changes as you go.

2. Discuss the impact of the war on the Union and Confederate "home fronts." Note economic issues, draft policy, and the roles of women.

3. Explain the considerations that led Lincoln to issue the Emancipation Proclamation. Discuss its overall impact on the war effort.

LECTURE OUTLINE

1. Lincoln's decision to issue an emancipation proclamation led directly to a **new birth of freedom**, while it radically enlarged the scope and purpose of the war and raised difficult questions concerning the future of the Union.

2. Both sides initially tried to sidestep the **issue of slavery**, but as time passed many northerners came to see a strike against it as a means of defeating the South.
   a. Slaves themselves helped force the issue by fleeing to Union lines, where they were allowed to remain, on grounds that they were **"contraband"** of war.
   b. Lincoln's efforts to persuade border state leaders to accept **"compensated emancipation"** met with obstinance and failure.
   c. Slave owner recalcitrance and calls from various advisors for tougher action led Lincoln to make a **decision for full emancipation**.

   (Show Transparency 16-01: Cartoon, Abe Lincoln's Last Card)

      i. Lincoln further reasoned that emancipation would enhance northern resolve and be well received by foreign nations.
      ii. Lincoln made his decision in July 1862 but was advised to **wait until** his armies had scored a **military success**, lest the policy look like a move of desperation.
   d. Lincoln called for 300,000 **new federal troops** and 300,000 more militiamen in the summer of 1862.
   e. General Lee, following upon his victory at second Bull Run, came north in September in a campaign that climaxed at the **battle of Antietam**.

   (Show Transparency 16-03: Map, Lee's Invasion of Maryland 1862; and Battle of Antietam, September 17, 1862)

      i. Numerous things went wrong for the Confederates; most notably, a copy of **Lee's orders** was found and given to General McClellan.
      ii. 23,000 combined casualties made September 17, 1862, the **bloodiest single-day of the war**.
   f. Though in many ways a draw, Lee's forces had retreated. The Union claimed victory, and Lincoln issued the **Emancipation Proclamation**.

3. Several developments made 1862–1863 a **winter of discontent**.
   a. Antietam encouraged Lincoln to remove McClellan. His replacement, Ambrose Burnside, launched a frontal assault on the heights of **Fredericksburg** that was repulsed with heavy casualties.
   b. The **Copperheads**, antiwar northern Democrats, called for the cessation of hostilities and recognition of southern independence.
   c. While the North struggled with low morale, southerners faced chronic food shortages, which at times exploded into **food riots**.
   d. In both the South (1862) and North (1863), wartime drafts were met with contempt by poorer elements, who resented exemptions afforded the wealthy.
      i. Southern **plantation owners were often excused** so as to keep watch over the slaves and prevent uprisings.

    ii. **Wealthy northerners could avoid the draft** by simply paying $300.00 as a commutation fee.

  e. Closer historical examination reveals that the war was **not exclusively** a **poor man's fight**, however.

4. The 37th Congress enacted three laws, which provided what historians have called a **blueprint for modern America**.

  a. The **Homestead Act** granted farmers 160 acre homesteads virtually free, provided they lived thereupon and made efforts to improve the land.

  b. The **Morrill Act** gave states thousands of acres of land with which to establish colleges.

  c. The **Pacific Railroad Act** granted land and loans to railroad companies so as to spur the grow of transcontinental lines.

  d. The war also offered many **opportunities to women**, which bolstered the fledgling women's rights movement.

    i. Their most notable achievement was likely the formation of the **United States Sanitary Commission**, which supplied nurses to army hospitals.

    ii. Some women served in war industries, others joined the civil service, still more served as spies, and **some actually enlisted** (posing as men).

5. The summer of 1863 is often considered the **high tide of the Confederacy**.

  a. Lee's defeat of Joseph Hooker at **Chancellorsville** that May owed to Lee's bold, aggressive reaction, and Hooker's loss of nerve.

  (Show Transparency 16-04: Map, Battle of Chancellorsville, May 2–6, 1863)

  b. Another Confederate invasion of the North climaxed from July 1 to 3, 1863, when Lee's army clashed with that of Hooker's replacement, George Meade, at **Gettysburg**, the greatest battle in American history.

  (Show Transparency 16-05: Map, Battle of Gettysburg, July 1–3, 1863)

    i. Thrice Lee attempted to dislodge Union forces from a series of hills east of the town—first attacking the northern and southern ends of the line, before assaulting the center in the quixotic **Pickett's charge**.

    ii. In three days of fighting, 50,000 men perished. Lee's army limped back to Virginia.

  c. Grant's successful conclusion of the **Vicksburg campaign** coincided with Lee's retreat from Gettysburg.

  (Show Transparency 16-06: Map, Vicksburg Campaign, April–July, 1863)

  d. Just a few months later, in September, Union forces under William Rosecrans captured **Chattanooga**.

    i. With reinforcements from the Army of Northern Virginia, Braxton Bragg was able to spring a trap on Rosecrans at **Chickamauga**.

  (Show Transparency 16-07: Map, Road to Chickamauga, June–September, 1863)

    ii. Lincoln reinforced Chattanooga with troops from Virginia and the Vicksburg campaign and **brought in Grant**, who drove Confederate forces off the surrounding heights in November.

6. The Emancipation Proclamation had reinforced calls for the enlistment of **black men in the Union armies**.
   a. Initially envisioned as garrison an supply forces, black regiments would themselves **push for the opportunity of combat**.
      i. In May and June 1863, black troops fought well in the campaign for **Port Hudson**.
      ii. The **54th Massachusetts** gallantly assaulted Fort Wagner (South Carolina) that July, suffering 50 percent casualties in a failed effort.
   b. Continued military victories were the principal factors in **confirming emancipation policy**.

7. Many southerners succumbed to defeatism during the trying winter of 1863–1864. More would do so in the following **"year of decision."**
   a. Confederate armies continued to resist, hoping that a **war of attrition** could tap antiwar sentiments, weaken northern wills, and prompt voters to oust Lincoln in the 1864 election in favor of a "peace Democrat."
   b. Grant, now general-in-chief, struck southward from Washington in early May. In two days of hellish fighting, the Confederates inflicted severe casualties on Grant's forces in the **"Wilderness."**

   (Show Transparency 16-08: Map, Battle of the Wilderness and Spotsylvania, May 5–12, 1864)

   c. **Grant did not retreat**, unlike earlier commanders. Instead he regrouped and again attempted to outflank Lee.
      i. In mid-May, assaults against Confederate entrenchments at **Spotsylvania** again produced high Union casualties.
      ii. On June 3, an ill-advised assault at **Cold Harbor** led to Union casualties reminiscent of Gettysburg.
   d. Grant eventually settled into what would become a nine-month siege of Petersburg, having suffered **65,000 total casualties** since May.
   e. In the West, **William Tecumsah Sherman** gradually pushed Joseph Johnston's forces back toward Atlanta.
      i. An impatient Jefferson Davis replaced Johnston with **John Bell Hood**, who launched three futile offensives, severely weakening his forces.
      ii. Sherman placed **Atlanta under siege**.

   (Show Transparency 16-09: Map, Campaign for Atlanta, May–September, 1864)

   f. The Confederate attrition strategy seemed to be working, evidenced not only by Democratic opposition but also by **growing dissent** among the Republicans.
      i. The **Democrats nominated George McClellan**, who called for an immediate cessation of hostilities.
      ii. **Lincoln himself despaired** that he would be badly beaten in his attempt at reelection, unless something drastic changed.
   g. Controversy over **prisoners of war** was further complicating matters for Lincoln.
      i. The most ghastly example of their suffering came at **Andersonville**, a "hellhole" in which soldiers died at a rate of more that one per day.

    ii. Lincoln resisted southern offers of **prisoner exchanges** until early 1865, however, largely because the South refused to include black troops in the proposals.

  h. A desperate Confederacy decided upon **recruiting slaves to fight**, but the war ended before any such regiments were organized.

8. An improved military situation eventually ensured the **reelection of Lincoln and the end of the Confederacy**.

  a. Sherman's **capture of Atlanta** from Hood's depleted forces in September was both a symbolic and substantive victory.

  b. Further Union success came in the **Shenandoah Valley**.

    i. Philip Sheridan sought not only to drive Jubal Early's forces from the valley but also to **deprive the Confederacy of the area's resources**.

    ii. Sheridan's men thoroughly destroyed the region and routed Early in a series of battles, climaxing at **Cedar Creek** in October.

  c. **The Confederate leadership resolved to keep fighting**. Sherman, who had long pondered the nature of war, resolved to convince them otherwise.

  d. **Sherman marched southward** 280 miles from Atlanta to Savannah, his 60,000 men wrecking almost everything in their path.

  e. Hood marched his forces northward, where he sacrificed the bulk of his men in attacks at **Franklin and Nashville**.

  f. The capture of **Fort Fisher** in January 1865 closed the Confederacy's last open port (Wilmington, North Carolina).

  (Show Transparency 16-10: Map, Hood's Tennessee Campaign, October–November 1864; and Nashville, December 15–16, 1864)

  g. Sherman's forces headed **northward through the Carolinas**, inflicting even more destruction than they had wrought upon Georgia.

  h. Grant, meanwhile, finally pressured Lee out of Richmond and Petersburg. Lee fled westward, only to have his remnant force cornered near **Appomattox**. On April 9, 1865, Lee surrendered.

  (Show Transparency 16-02: Graph, Comparative Strength of Union and Confederate Armies)

  i. Northern celebrations soon turned to mourning, however, following the **assassination of Lincoln** on April 14.

American Album: The Fruits of War

Conclusion: The Civil War resolved two fundamental questions. The first involved the elimination of slavery. The second involved the superiority of federal authority to that of the states. Such resolution came at a cost of over 600,000 lives.

TEACHING RESOURCES

The Civil War—episodes four through nine—by Ken Burns offers an award-winning account of the war's middle and closing years. PBS Video (62 minutes, 95 minutes, 70 minutes, 72 minutes, 69 minutes, and 68 minutes, respectively).

The Red Badge of Courage is a feature film of Stephen Crane's classic novel, directed by John Huston and starring Audie Murphy. Filmic Archives (69 minutes).

Smithsonian's *Great Battles of the Civil War* is a six-part series that offers narration by James M. McPherson and documentation of each major battle of the war. Filmic Archives.

Royal Federal Blues provides the most comprehensive account of African-American participation in the Civil War. Filmic Archives (30 minutes).

Glory is a feature film, starring Denzel Washington, about the 54th Massachusetts Infantry. Filmic Archives (120 minutes).

Lincoln is a four-part series about the president. Filmic Archives (240 minutes total).

Great Generals of the South focuses on Robert E. Lee and Stonewall Jackson. Filmic Archives (60 minutes).

Chapter 17
Reconstruction, 1863–1877

CHAPTER SUMMARY

From the beginning of the Civil War, the North fought to "reconstruct" the Union. By December 1863, President Lincoln had developed an amnesty and Reconstruction plan for the nation. Lincoln offered amnesty to most Confederates—exceptions having been high-ranking civilian and military officials, who were required to take a loyalty oath to the United States and accept the end of slavery. When 10 percent of a state's voters (by 1860 counts) had taken the oath of loyalty, a new state government could be established. Louisiana, Arkansas, and Tennessee—states the Union Army controlled—followed Lincoln's plan.

This swift and mild Reconstruction plan, however, greatly upset radical Republicans, such as Thaddeus Stevens and Charles Sumner, who wanted southerners to pay for the rebellion and sought political rights for blacks. Furthermore, many congressional Republicans insisted that Reconstruction was a legislative matter, not the business of the president. They answered Lincoln's plan with the Wade-Davis Bill of July 1864, a plan calling for a tougher amnesty policy. Lincoln's veto of the bill deepened the division within his own party and made Reconstruction more problematic.

Before the president could issue further Reconstruction policies, the war ended and Lincoln was assassinated. At first, the new president, Andrew Johnson, seemed to endorse the radical Republican views on Reconstruction, but in May 1865, he offered his own. Like his predecessor, Johnson proposed amnesty to most former Confederates through the use of the loyalty oath. Exceptions to this general amnesty were, again, the highest-ranking Confederate leaders, but to this group Johnson added a new category: anyone who owned taxable property worth $20,000 or more—in other words, wealthy plantation owners. Such people, whom Johnson blamed for causing the war, would receive amnesty only by making a personal application to Johnson himself. To implement each state's Reconstruction, Johnson proposed to appoint a provisional governor who would call for an election of delegates to draw up a new state constitution. Only those white men who had received amnesty could vote or serve as delegates. The new constitution had to repudiate the Confederacy and comply with the U.S. Constitution.

To the growing dismay of moderate and radical Republicans, southern whites in the summer and fall of 1865 followed the parts of Johnson's plan that they liked and ignored the parts they disliked. Southern defiance seemed on the verge of becoming southern rebellion once again. Johnson undermined his own plan by pardoning thousands of former Confederate leaders and plantation owners. Southern voters then horrified northerners by electing some former leaders of the rebellion to Congress.

The fear that southern whites planned to reenslave blacks arose when the new state legislatures enacted the Black Codes in the fall of 1865. While granting some new rights to former slaves, these laws imposed a second-class citizenship on blacks that denied them the ability to vote, to serve on a jury, to testify against whites, and, in one state, to own land. The codes' definition of vagrancy enabled whites to force blacks to work on farms and plantations, creating a situation that seemed very much like slavery.

Already active in dealing with southern labor and racial problems was the federal agency known as the Freedmen's Bureau. Created in March 1865, its purpose was to ease the transition of blacks and whites from a system of slavery to one of free labor. It provided protection to former slaves, set up and supervised labor contracts between whites and blacks, and attempted, in a variety of ways, to reconstruct the southern economy and end the postwar chaos. Private agencies, such as missionary groups from the North, also offered aid to former slaves by setting up schools and hiring teachers to staff them.

When Congress reconvened in December 1865, the Republican majority refused to seat the representatives elected under Johnson's Reconstruction plan and struck at the Black Codes by strengthening the Freedmen's Bureau's power to set them aside. To protect blacks further, Congress passed the Civil Rights Act of 1866, which gave them citizenship and equal protection under the law. Johnson's vetoes of the new Freedmen's Bureau bill and the Civil Rights Act—and Congress's override of these vetoes—revealed not only a deep rift between president and Congress but also a threat to any presidential control over Reconstruction.

To culminate this first battle with the president, Congress created its own Reconstruction policies in the form of the Fourteenth Amendment. In addition to giving citizenship to former slaves, the proposed amendment prohibited states from depriving "any person of life, liberty, or property without due process of law" and from denying to any person "the equal protection of the laws." Other provisions urged southern states to give black males the right to vote, disqualified ex-Confederate leaders from holding office, repudiated the Confederate war debt, and gave Congress power to enforce the amendment. When Tennessee ratified the Fourteenth Amendment, the only one of the former Confederate states to do so, Congress pronounced it reconstructed.

White race riots in the summer of 1866 and Johnson's own clumsy campaigning on behalf of congressional candidates ensured the collapse of presidential Reconstruction and paved the way for Congress's more complete plan. When issued in March of 1867, Congress's plan reimposed military control over the remaining ten unreconstructed states, ordered generals to register voters for elections to choose delegates to state constitutional conventions, enfranchised all males over age twenty-one, and disfranchised (temporarily) former Confederate leaders. When a state had a new constitution that gave equal political rights to all adult males and civil rights to all citizens, and had ratified the Fourteenth Amendment, civilian rule would be restored and newly elected congressional representatives would be seated. This plan brought the Republican Party into power in the South, infuriating former southern leaders who soon charged that the new state governments were being run by "carpetbaggers" (northerners), "scalawags" (southern white Unionists), and former slaves ("Negro rule").

The power struggle between the president and Congress climaxed when Johnson challenged the Tenure of Office Act, which had taken away his power to fire his own cabinet officials. The House impeached Johnson in February 1868 on violation of this law and for failing to maintain the proper relationship between Congress and the presidency. Johnson's lawyers exploited a loophole in the Tenure of Office Act and forced senators to consider removing the president because of his failure to cooperate with Congress. By one vote, Johnson escaped removal from office.

Despite white opposition, and even violence from groups such as the Ku Klux Klan, new state governments in the South pressed forward with reforms that included universal male suffrage and the creation of statewide public education. For states that refused to implement the congressional plan, ratification of the Fifteenth Amendment became an additional requirement for Reconstruction after its passage by Congress in 1869. This constitutional change prohibited states from using race, color, or previous condition of servitude as a reason for withholding voting rights.

Ulysses S. Grant won the presidential election in 1868, marking the beginning of the end for Reconstruction policies. During Grant's two terms, corruption flourished inside and outside his administration. Scandals involving Grant's close friends, cabinet officials, members of Congress, and state and local political leaders, shocked (and titillated) the nation. Cries for civil service reform arose, leading finally to the passage of the Pendleton Act in 1883. Financial fluctuations and speculation brought on the Panic of 1873, a depression that lasted until 1878.

Racist and violent southern whites continued to fight against Republican control in the South. Despite efforts to crack down on violence by white supremacists, Congress restored political rights to former Confederate leaders, and Grant continued to withdraw federal troops from the South. The Democratic Party came into power once again, and former slaves feared that the right to vote and other newfound rights were imperiled. With the so-called Compromise of 1877, the Republicans turned over to the Democrats the remaining southern states that they controlled in return for continued Republican control of the presidency. The Supreme Court's narrow interpretation of Reconstruction laws and amendments further signaled that Reconstruction was over.

LIBERTY, EQUALITY, POWER: A THEMATIC BRAID

The question of power arose in the era of the Reconstruction concerning how to give political and economic power to former slaves. Also problematic was the prevention of former Confederates from regaining power and, possibly, starting a new rebellion. Republicans believed that barring former Confederate leaders from office and enfranchising black adult males would give former slaves the political clout to protect themselves and, with white allies, the power to put the Republican Party into control of the South—the only sure way of preventing another rebellion. Eventually, these ideas took the form of the Fourteenth and Fifteenth Amendments, which became the cornerstones not only of the Reconstruction but of protection of the individual from state abuses of civil rights.

From the cavalier attitude toward Johnson's Reconstruction plan to the passage of the Black Codes and to resistance to congressional Reconstruction policies, southern whites showed that they deeply resented the shift in social and political power that Reconstruction seemed to provide. They fought back with propaganda ("Negro rule," "carpetbaggers," "scalawags") and violence (Ku Klux Klan, Knights of the White Camellia, etc.).

The establishment of the Freedmen's Bureau and the ratification of the Fourteenth and Fifteenth Amendments marked an enormous gain in federal power at the expense of the states. The bureau was arguably the first national welfare agency, and the amendments put the federal government into position to protect the civil liberties of the individual from state abuse.

The other power struggle of the era was between the executive and legislative branches of the federal government. Each claimed the power to control Reconstruction, but Congress ultimately gained the advantage by refusing to seat men elected to Congress under the presidential plan and by impeaching Andrew Johnson. The Senate's refusal to remove Johnson from office revealed that many senators were uneasy about changing the balance of power among the branches of the federal government, but Congress still emerged from the impeachment trial firmly in control of Reconstruction.

IDENTIFICATIONS

Proclamation of
   Reconstruction
William Marcy Tweed
Credit Mobilier
Pendleton Act
Treaty of Washington (1871)

Amnesty and Whiskey Ring
Thaddeus Stevens
Radical Republicans
Charles Sumner
Wade-Davis Bill
Andrew Johnson

Fenians
carpetbaggers
scalawags
"Negro rule"
Lyman Trumbull
Fourteenth Amendment
Civil Rights Cases
Mississippi Plan
"Bulldozing"
Samuel J. Tilden
Rutherford B. Hayes
Compromise of 1877
Horace Greeley
Reconstruction Acts of 1867

Johnathan Gibbs
Black Codes
Freedmen's Bureau
sharecropper
"40 acres and a mule"
Tenure of Office Act
Edwin M. Stanton
Ku Klux Klan
Hamburg Massacre
Fifteenth Amendment
Ulysses S. Grant
Jay Cooke
Colfax Massacre
National Union Party

CHRONOLOGY

1863	Lincoln announces his Reconstruction plan.
1864	Louisiana, Arkansas, and Tennessee follow Lincoln's Reconstruction plan for readmittance to the Union.
	Wade-Davis Bill passed by Congress; Lincoln kills it through pocket veto.
1865	Freedmen's Bureau established by Congress.
	Andrew Johnson becomes president.
	Johnson issues his Reconstruction plan and readmits the rest of the former Confederate states to the Union.
	Southern states enact the Black Codes.
	Congress refuses to seat southern Congressmen elected under Johnson's Reconstruction plan.
1866	Freedmen's Bureau is extended and given more power.
	Congress approves the Fourteenth Amendment.
	Race riots break out in Memphis and New Orleans.
	Republicans increase their majority in congressional elections.
1867	Congressional Reconstruction plan is passed over Johnson's veto.
	Tenure of Office Act is enacted to trim Johnson's power to interfere in Reconstruction.
1868	Most southern states are readmitted to Congress under the congressional plan.
	Andrew Johnson is impeached but not convicted.
	Fourteenth Amendment is ratified.
	Ulysses S. Grant wins election as president.
1869	Congress passes the Fifteenth Amendment, ratified in 1870.
1871	Ku Klux Klan Act is enacted and enforced in part of South Carolina.
1872	Liberal Republicans defect from the party.
	Grant wins reelection.

1873	Economic depression begins with the Panic.
1875	"Whiskey Ring" and other scandals befoul the Grant administration.
1877	Rutherford B. Hayes becomes president after a disputed election. Compromise of 1877 removes last federal soldiers from the South.

THEMATIC TOPICS FOR ENRICHMENT

1. How did Andrew Johnson's background, especially his experiences as a prewar politician, affect his Reconstruction position?

2. Discuss the Black Codes and why Republicans found them so objectionable.

3. Explain the role of the Freedmen's Bureau in the South and discuss the labor and racial problems with which it tried to deal.

4. Why did Congress and Andrew Johnson part ways on Reconstruction policies? What events in early 1866 worsened relations between the two?

5. Discuss the provisions of the Fourteenth Amendment and explain why the amendment became such an important guarantor of civil rights.

6. Discuss the events leading to the impeachment of Andrew Johnson. Why did the Senate fail to remove him from office?

7. Discuss the role of the Ku Klux Klan and other terrorist groups during Reconstruction.

8. Discuss the Compromise of 1877 and why it marked the end of Reconstruction.

GEOGRAPHY OBJECTIVES

1. With reference to the map on page 597, note the only state to have a black majority at its constitutional convention. Which state had equal representation of whites and blacks?

2. With further reference to the text of pages 601–602, discuss how the map on page 597 challenges notions of the southern Republicans as being a predominantly black party.

3. As you examine the map on page 600, note how the Reconstruction experience of Tennessee differed dramatically from those of the other southern states. Be sure to consult the text concerning how the Fourteenth and Fifteenth Amendments fit into this equation.

4. Use the map on page 609 to compute what the final vote tallies would have been if any of the three "disputed" states (Florida, Louisiana, South Carolina) had been counted for Tilden. Then, perhaps with reference to the map on page 597, note the final vote count if southern Republicans were not "bulldozed" out of power. Finally, discuss the importance of New York to Tilden's claims. Why, do you think, did New York vote Democratic?

SUGGESTED ESSAY TOPICS

1. Compare and contrast the Reconstruction policies (noting attitudes toward both former slaves and ex-Confederates) of Abraham Lincoln, Andrew Johnson, and the Radical Republicans.

2. Explain what was meant by the terms *carpetbagger, scalawag,* and *Negro rule.* How true was the propaganda against Republican-controlled state governments in the South?

3. Assess U.S. Grant's two terms as president. What did he accomplish? What were his failures?

LECTURE OUTLINE

1. From the beginning of the Civil War, the North fought with **Reconstruction** in mind. The precise meaning of that word, however, varied among individuals, and changed as the war continued.

2. Lincoln's **Proclamation of Amnesty and Reconstruction** seemed, to many Republicans, both too lenient toward former Confederates and insufficient in guaranteeing the rights and liberties of former slaves.
   a. When certain Confederate state governments reorganized under this plan, they denied blacks the vote and enacted restrictive labor laws that **seemed a veritable return to slavery.**

   (Show Transparency 17-01: Thomas Nast Cartoon, "This is a white man's government.")

   b. Radical Republicans came to support tougher policies epitomized in the **Wade-Davis Bill.**

3. **Andrew Johnson** became president upon Lincoln's assassination.
   a. Johnson expressed no love for the planter class but was a **white supremacist** who aimed to deny blacks the fruits of Reconstruction.
      i. Under Johnson's plans, the southern states defiantly **elected prominent Confederate officials** to office.
      ii. Johnson also granted **special pardons** to many of those "aristocrats" whom he had earlier vowed to punish.
   b. Even more alarming to Radical Republicans was the establishment of the **Black Codes,** which relegated blacks to second-class citizenship.
   c. The war had left the **southern economy** in chaos. Planters had no labor, and ex-slaves often had neither land nor work.
   d. The **Freedmen's Bureau** sought to establish labor contracts between landowners and the former slaves.
      i. Proposals to provide **land for the landless** through confiscation of plantations failed to reach fruition.
      ii. Eventually, a new system of **sharecropping** emerged.
   f. The Freedmen's Bureau was more successful in providing **educational opportunities for blacks.**

4. By the time Congress met in 1865, the Republican majority had resolved to challenge Johnson with **new Reconstruction policies.**
   a. **Johnson showed contempt** for Congressional initiatives.
   b. Congress passed a civil rights bill and another expanding the Freedmen's Bureau's powers, **overriding presidential vetoes.**
   c. More dramatically, Congress sent to the states the **Fourteenth Amendment,** which vastly expanded federal powers to prevent state violations of civil rights.

    d. Johnson's obstinacy and courting of disgraced Democrats were pivotal factors in a sweeping radical Republican victory in the **1866 congressional elections**.

    e. Given a three-to-one majority, the Republican Congress passed the **Reconstruction Acts of 1867**.

        i. They enfranchised black males, disfranchised certain ex-Confederates, and sent the army south for **enforcement**.

        ii. Some **735,000 enfranchised black voters** became the backbone of the Republican party in the South, which took control of southern state governments.

5. Johnson did everything he could to stop Congressional Reconstruction, provoking considerable ire. His firing of the Secretary of War was the final straw, which convinced the House to vote for **impeachment**.

    a. A few Republicans were persuaded to **acquit** the president, sparing him from impeachment **by one vote**. Johnson was left politically impotent, however.

    b. **Majority Republican state conventions** enacted universal male suffrage and mandated statewide public schools for both races.

    c. With ratification of the **Fifteenth Amendment** in 1870, the Constitution became color-blind for the first time in history.

    d. Ulysses S. Grant, who had openly broken with Johnson, won the **1868 election**.

(Show Transparency 17-02: Map, Black and White Participation in Constitutional Conventions, 1867–1868)

6. The **Grant administration** is usually branded a failure, owing to widespread corruption among presidential subordinates.

    a. In reality, several government agencies made real progress in establishing a more professional and qualified **civil service**.

    b. The administration also achieved some **foreign policy** success by ameliorating tensions with Great Britain and Canada.

    c. Blacks comprised 80 percent of southern Republican voters yet held only 15 to 20 percent of elected positions. The **myth of "ignorant" black politicians** is patently false.

    d. **Carpetbaggers** (northern whites who moved to the South) did occupy a disproportionate number of political offices, but most were not unscrupulous, as southern myths would have it.

    e. **Scalawags** (southern native white Republicans) came largely from areas with traditional hostility to the southern planter aristocracy.

    f. While the Fifteenth Amendment seemed to many a victory for Reconstruction, there was **no peace in the South**.

(Show Transparency 17-03: Map, Reconstruction in the South)

    g. The most potent weapon of the Democrat arsenal was violence, epitomized by the **Ku Klux Klan**.

        i. One Klan goal was to keep blacks consigned to second-class citizenship. The **burning of schools** represents but one example of this intention.

        ii. The Klan also strove to destroy the Republican party by **terrorizing voters**.

    h. Grant staved off the challenge of "Liberal Republican" Horace Greeley to win **reelection in 1872**, but Greeley's calls to abandon Reconstruction struck a responsive chord with many northerners.

        i. To make matters worse, **panic on Wall Street in 1873** plunged the economy into a five-year recession.

7. Economic anguish, and a growing weariness with the seemingly endless turmoil of southern politics, turned many northern voters against the Republican party and prompted **retreat from Reconstruction**.

   a. Democratic tactics of coercing white Republicans and intimidating black voters threw the **Mississippi election of 1875**.

   b. The **Supreme Court**, meanwhile, ruled against many aspects of civil rights legislation, even challenging the Fourteenth and Fifteenth Amendments via narrow interpretation.

   c. The **election of 1876** between Samuel Tilden and Rutherford Hayes was held amidst Democratic attempts to "bulldoze" black voters into submission.

   d. The candidates polled nearly equal votes. But three southern states experienced **disputed returns** owing to widespread "bulldozing."

   e. Congress had to appoint a special committee to break the deadlock by hammering out the **Compromise of 1877**.

      i. To avert crisis, the Republicans agreed to provide economic help to the South and to **end "bayonet rule."**

      ii. The Democrats agreed to accept **Hayes as president**.

   f. Without federal troop support, the southern Republican party collapsed. Thus the Compromise marks the **end of Reconstruction**.

American Album: Cartoons for Freedom

Conclusion: Reconstruction had both reincorporated former Confederate states into the Union and destroyed slavery. But continued inequities relegated the newly freed slaves into second-class citizenship, wherein most would remain for nearly another century.

TEACHING RESOURCES

Opening of the West is a documentary on the Reconstruction and westward expansion. Filmic Archives (53 minutes).

America Grows Up covers the period from 1850 to c. 1900, focusing on manufacturing, foreign policy, and the shift from a rural to an urban society. Filmic Archives (53 minutes).

The Klan: A Legacy of Hate in America provides an overview of the first 120 years of the organization. Filmic Archives (30 minutes).

The Iron Road details the building and completion of the transcontinental railroad. PBS Video (60 minutes).

Core Concept Video
Instructor's Guide

INTRODUCTION

Harcourt Brace's Core Concept video package to accompany *Liberty, Equality, Power: A History of the American People* is an innovative teaching tool created so that students can learn by connecting the written word with visual images. The two videos that comprise our package do not replace the textbook; they enhance key text concepts. The subjects selected for the videos relate directly to the underlying theme of the textbook—liberty, equality, power—and how these concepts interact to drive the American experience. With this goal in mind, we selected 16 topics that fit our criteria and serve to "flesh out" central issues raised in the textbook.

These subjects appear as video segments, arranged chronologically with eight segments on each video. Several topics that have a close relationship to the central theme of the textbook receive special emphasis. Chief among these are the issues of slavery and the African-American struggle for liberty and equality; the Constitution and the never-ending endeavors to find the proper balance of power that will ensure liberty and equality for all citizens; and the continual influx of immigrants and the movements of migrants in their attempts to acquire liberty, equality, and security in a new home.

One video covers American history up to 1877, and the second examines America since 1863. *Liberty, Equality, Power* contains five sections, and the videos conform loosely to these sections. This parallel structure allowed us to involve one of our authors in every video segment that corresponds to material addressed by each in the textbook. The involvement of the textbook authors is a very important part of this video package. One author introduces each of the 16 video segments and brings a sense of expertise and immediacy to this ancillary.

Each video segment begins with an introduction by the textbook author who briefly discusses what follows and how it relates to the corresponding chapters in the textbook. Concept clues prior to the running video footage alert the viewer to vital information in the video. These clues are followed by approximately 10 minutes of running video that focuses on a subject corresponding to the textbook themes. Each video segment ends with a series of questions that take the viewer from video image to textbook concept. Text stills that foster critical thinking and stimulate concept recall appear following the segment-ending questions.

Since the videos are designed to complement *Liberty, Equality, Power*, they are of the greatest value when used in conjunction with the textbook. This use can be accomplished in a number of ways. Use the videos in the classroom, have your students view them at home, or both. Most students have access to a VCR, and the videos are inexpensive. When covering a chapter that corresponds to one of the video segments, assign the chapter and the video segment prior to lecture. Then illustrate your lecture with the video, integrating it into your discussion and focusing on the subject as an illustration of the core concept. You can further utilize the video package by choosing some of the questions contained in this Instructor's Guide. Your use of the videos in the classroom and/or your posing of questions about the video material in lectures or on exams encourages your students to use the videos at home.

The videos are also excellent lecture launchers. Prior to a lecture whose topic relates well to a certain video segment, you might wish to introduce the lecture with the video. Each video segment runs less than 15 minutes, leaving adequate lecture time. We have also had several class test sites in which the instructor has chosen to employ the video as a summation tool following a lecture. Both are very useful means of integrating the videos into the classroom. You might decide to make the videos available to your students on an optional basis by ordering copies for the bookstore or by placing your copy on reserve in the library. Whatever means you select, these videos, in tandem with *Liberty, Equality, Power*, will give your students an improved understanding of the American experience.

This Guide provides you with information and suggestions for using the videos in the classroom. First, a brief Overview introduces the video topic and gives insights into the content of the video. This overview is followed by Classroom Use of Video Segments, which provides ideas for classroom discussion. The Concluding Questions section includes one or more essay test questions. Video to Text Issues focus on questions that tie together both *Liberty, Equality, Power* and the video segment. Selected Classroom Exercises are included for several video segments and suggest classroom or group projects. The Related Films section provides a brief list of films that elaborate on the topic covered in the video segment.

We believe that this unique video package serves as a marvelous teaching tool that helps bring American history to life. We offer this guide as a compass for using videos designed to directly complement a textbook. If, while using this video package along with *Liberty, Equality, Power,* you discover teaching strategies that enhance the classroom experience for your students, we welcome your ideas.

Access Codes to Videos

Volume I: America to 1877

When Old Worlds Collide
(access 00:00:43)
Slavery in New York City: Unearthing the Slave Trade
(access 00:14:36)
Newcomers to a New World: Contributions and Controversies
(access 00:27:18)
To Make This Land Prosper: Agriculture and Westward Settlement
(access 00:44:24)
Let the End Be Legitimate: The Supreme Court, the National Government, and the National Economy
(access 00:54:13)
Art, Romanticism, and Culture: Connections East and West
(access 01:19:37)
Constitutional Principles and Race Relations: The Beginning
(access 01:33:18)
Frederick Douglass: The Lesson of the Hour (I)
(access 01:59:17)

Volume I: America to 1877

Suggestions for Instructional Use of Video Segments

corresponding to Chapters 1–6

When Old Worlds Collide

Overview

When Old Worlds Collide focuses on the theme of power as it describes pre-Columbian Mesoamerica and the impact of the Spanish conquest on the Aztecs. The video segment concentrates on two primary topics: first, the pre-Aztec civilization at Teotihuacán, and, second, the story of the Spanish conquest of Mexico. The running video begins with views of modern Mexico City and then moves to clips ranging from the 1910 excavation of the Pyramid of the Sun at Teotihuacán to present work on the site. Archaeologists John Reece Davis and Esther Pasztore describe the size and complexity of the pre-Aztec civilization. Both stress the power of ideology in building this vast civilization that had great influence on the later Aztecs. The remaining part of the excerpt tells the traditional story of the conquest of the Aztecs by Cortés and his small band of soldiers. Scenes from the Aztec Codex are used to illustrate this event, ending with the Spanish victory and the defeat of the Aztec nation.

Classroom Use of Video Segment

Discuss the surprising nature of the archaeological evidence found at Teotihuacán.

Focus on the degree of influence that Teotihuacán had on the Aztecs. Inquire about examples of earlier civilizations having significant effects on later cultures.

Discuss the power of myths and legends in making the Aztecs more vulnerable to conquest.

Concluding Questions

The video makes only brief reference to the role of disease in the conquest of the Aztecs, yet we know, as the textbook points out, that the power of biological forces had a profound impact on the indigenous people of the Americas who had little resistance to the communicable diseases brought by the Europeans. Ask your class to draw from both video and textbook in order to explain the reasons why these commonplace European illnesses proved so devastating to the Aztecs as well as other native Americans.

The power of religion proved essential in the swift conquest and pacification of the Americas. Have your students explain the reasons for this rapid conversion to Christianity and what elements were essential to this phenomenon.

Recent examination of the Spanish conquest of the Americas has questioned the role of traditional interpretations, such as advanced technology or a more sophisticated sociopolitical organization. Have your students discuss the most recent interpretations of the role played by biological forces and by ideology and explain why these are more credible.

Video to Text Issues

Why was the experience of Cortés in Mexico different from that of Columbus in the Caribbean?

Compare and contrast the Spanish experience in Mexico with that of the Inca conquest in Peru.

What factors made the Spanish and English encounters in the Americas different?

Suggested Classroom Exercises

List examples of contemporary "cultural baggage" that originated from the European encounter/conquest of the Americas. What aspects are positive and which are negative?

Related Films

"Columbus's World" The second half of this initial film in the series *Columbus and the Age of Discovery* provides a good overview of medieval Europe and explores the motivations for exploration in the fifteenth century.

The Sword and the Cross An excellent account of the impact of the conquistadores and the friars on the Mesoamerican cultures, offering new interpretations.

The Columbian Exchange A visual analysis of the effects of this phenomenon on modern life, this film enables the viewer to see the direct connection and influence of this pattern.

Slavery in New York City: Unearthing the Slave Trade

Overview

The 1992 discovery of an African-American burial ground located in the heart of New York City opened up a new chapter in the city's history. Archaeologist Warren Barbour stresses how important this site is to understanding the role played by slaves in the development of colonial New York City. The city had the second largest slave population in the colonies and 40 percent of the city's total population was of African origin. Here we see a demonstration of the ambivalent relationship between liberty, equality, and power with slaves in colonial New York participating fully in urban life and helping to build the commercial base of the city. Bioanthropologist Michael Blakey describes why slavery gave African Americans a unique history. Views of the port of Minna and an old slave fort on the African Gold Coast show the connections between the slave trade and the growth of prosperity in the Americas. Archaeologist Christopher DeCourse, an expert on the slave trade, explains why little is known about the African origins of those enslaved. The video ends with a commentary on slave life in colonial New York City, including the infamous 1712 slave revolt. Present-day excavation of the burial site promises to yield more information about the role of African Americans in building the largest city in this country.

Classroom Use of Video Segment

Have your class make a list of reasons why the New York City burial site is so important. Discuss each reason in class.

Discuss with your students why African migration to the Americas was so different from that of other groups. You might want to extend this exercise by focusing on the role of various aspects of power in creating these differences.

Have your students analyze the problems created by slaveholding during colonial times and how this form of power affected individuals' liberty and equality.

Concluding Questions

This 1992 historical find resulted in the reopening of debate regarding the interpretation of roles played by African Americans in the colonial experience. Describe the insights provided by the work completed on this site.

The new evidence of slave life in colonial New York City uncovered at the burial site has provided material for diverse interpretations of the colonial period. Point out to your students how scholarly research continues to change our views of the past, and then discuss what implications this research holds for "conventional wisdom," traditional interpretations, and revisionist history.

Video to Text Issues

How are contemporary issues such as racism or power politics connected to new historical evidence such as this burial site?

In what ways can history be used or abused to support political views, social issues, or economic developments?

Suggested Classroom Exercises

Employ a pretest to gauge knowledge and preconceptions about colonial slavery, especially as it related to the northern colonial urban environment. Use an open-ended post-test to measure reactions and change.

Related Films

"Origins" from *In Search of the Dream* An exploration of the impact of slavery on African-American life and culture from 1619 to the late twentieth century.

Digging for Slaves: The Excavation of American Slave Sites   By describing three colonial slave-quarter sites, Middleburg Plantation, Monticello, and colonial Williamsburg, the viewer is given an accurate and surprising picture of slave life. The Monticello segment is especially useful for exploring racial attitudes that slavery engendered.

Suggestions for Instructional Use of Video Segments

corresponding to Chapters 7–12

Newcomers to a New World: Contributions and Controversies

Overview

Paul Johnson, the author of Chapters 7–12 of *Liberty, Equality, Power*, tells students how immigrants from Germany and Scandinavia moved to the West and established commercial market farming. This is also the primary focus of this video segment; the video coverage corresponds particularly well to sections in Chapters 9, 10, and 11. Both the video and Professor Johnson detail the transformation of the cities during the market revolution and specifically point to the availability of cheap labor as a key to development. Both note the role of immigrants in developing urban sports, especially blood sports such as prizefighting. Finally, they explain the role immigrants played in the political and reform controversies of antebellum years. This discussion includes examination of why the Whigs played to nativist's fears and how the issue of public schools and temperance became "immigrant" issues as well. The social effects of, and response to, immigrants are also covered well.

Classroom Use of Video Segment

The video and textbook point out that both appeals to change or resistance to change have often been cloaked in the language of liberty or equality, or the use of the threat of abusive power to scare citizens. Political parties have been using these tactics throughout our history, as have "reformers" and interest groups.

Students can identify the political use of these appeals, and especially their use of the book's themes. Consider Federalists versus Jeffersonians, Democrats versus Whigs. For extension, instructors can have students carry this political consideration on through the rest of the course, right up to the alarmist and "patriotic" appeals heard today. Students can choose different reform movements (i.e., education, temperance, literacy, voting) and examine how movements use and misuse these themes. Be sure to have them make a similar examination of the arguments used by those "opposing reform." Have students consider special interest groups (bankers, monopolists, nativists, or others) and how they use these themes. Why would groups use these appeals, what legitimate concerns might they have for United States society, and why could they not see more than one side of the issues?

United States society changes in many ways, but does this always translate into better things for the American people?

Rural society enters the market economy. Does this process provide farmers and their families more power over their lives? Does it increase their equality vis-a-vis their neighbors, or increase their liberty and ability to advance further, or hurt them just as much?

Cities grow as the nation becomes first commercialized and then industrialized. This growth increases the number of factory and industrial jobs available for men and women. Do these changes mean greater equality for all urban residents? Are they all empowered to the same extent? Have your students consider living quarters, political power, purchasing power, and distribution of income.

For greater challenge and critical thinking, have students consider whether the new industrialists actually promoted "republican virtue" by developing the factory system (using the ideas of John Kasson) or were instead creating the horrors Melville depicted in "The Maids of Tartarus."

You may also want your students to consider applying the video segment on farming to these ideas.

Racism, sexism, and greed all interfere with the acquisition of equality, liberty, or the distribution of power. Yet these are part of the human condition, and the history of the United States. Students should be able to identify how these issues interplayed with the themes of the textbook. They should also be able to trace their existence from the first days of the Republic to the present.

Suggested Classroom Exercises

For instructors who like comparative history, this segment allows comparisons between the Old World and the New. Consider how industrialism affected each continent or how land ownership laws affected the development of political systems.

This video segment can be used as a lead-in for urban history. Look at the changes brought by immigrant populations and rapidly growing urban populations. What were the conditions like in these cities? What city services that we take for granted were not available? How did slums develop?

Focus on family histories. This segment traces orally the lives of several immigrants. Students can be encouraged to go home and get oral history from family members, learning to personalize and apply United States history to themselves.

This video lets instructors start examining nativism, the fear of subversion, conspiracy theories, and scapegoating in United States history. This attitude can, unfortunately, be traced all the way to the present day. Alternatively, instructors could use this video to begin a discussion of multiculturalism and help students understand how diverse our national heritage is.

Related Films

Ethnic Notions One of the few videos available today on immigrants, this film deals with immigrant life and singularity, how this differed from the customs and traits of the established residents of the United States. It also touches on the nativist reaction to the apparent "clannishness" of the immigrants. Can be used to expand the study of immigrant life beyond the Irish.

Five Points Examines the legendary (or dreaded) Five Points district in New York City. This is where immigrants were herded, and from where other citizens claimed all lawlessness, disorder, and machine politics spewed forth. Another option from the detail on Boston is provided in the video clip. New York was the arrival location for the most immigrants, so using this video is very appropriate.

In addition, instructors can make use of three video indexes. The R. R. Bowker Company publishes two of them:

> *The Educational Film & Video Locator of the Consortium of College and University Media Centers*, two volumes.
> *The AV Marketplace Film and Video Finder*, three volumes by the National Information Center for Educational Media.

To Make This Land Prosper: Agriculture and Westward Settlement

Overview

Paul Johnson's textbook coverage links well with this video segment, in particular, early sections of Chapter 7 and Chapter 9 and throughout Chapter 12. There is marvelous treatment of the "Farmers' Republic," households, work patterns, the social organization of communities and standards of living for rural areas. In addition, Johnson explains in the text how the natives are forced off their land to allow American farmers in. The text also makes the connection between Henry Clay's idea of regional agricultural specialization and the market economy. Detail is given on how the yeomen farmers in the Northeast and Old Northwest shift from self-sufficiency to becoming cogs in the free market economy. If you want to do something more, reinforce the connection between the westward movement, agriculture, and the marketplace.

Classroom Use of Video Segment

Paul Johnson in *Liberty, Equality, Power* points out the importance of the agrarian republic lifestyle to the Founding Fathers. Key to this ideal were the twin features of property ownership and citizenship, along with the duties and responsibilities that come along with both to be a good citizen of the new nation. This ideal provided for a well-ordered society where people knew their roles. Instructors can note the connection between property and liberty and have students extend the use of this ideal, and the duties (if any) still associated with this ideal, right up to the present day.

Have your students consider that, in this society, equality and power were for white, male property owners only, and consequently meant powerlessness and inequality for everyone else. How can students justify this, or have them explain how citizens then balanced this with the ideas of constitutional rights and a republican form of government.

Consider using the power theme in the context that every major expansion across this continent was done in the name of providing more farmland for the "yeomen farmers" of the agrarian myth.

Consider how rural society changed with the rise of the market economy. What does this mean for the future of the perfect "republican form of government" if the independent yeoman farmer just becomes a cog in the free market economy? What tensions could this cause in society?

Use this video to demonstrate and connect the above issues.

The textbook provides considerable insight into the lives of women and children and how families worked, played, and struggled in both urban and rural communities. Their lives changed as the United States moved from a simple agrarian republic towards industrialism.

What were the limits of liberty, power, and equality for women and children? Who or what determined these limits?

Did any of these groups become more empowered as society changed? For example, how did women working in the Lowell Mills change their status in society?

What steps did women take to improve their lives, their families' lives, or society around them? How did these actions fit into the ideas of liberty, power, and equality?

Videos on immigration and farming life both describe the lives of families in real terms and not just clichés.

Suggested Classroom Exercises

The Turner Frontier Thesis may be discussed with this video. How do its arguments seem true in this video, and what fallacies are obvious as well? This discussion may be extended to include later times.

The yeoman farmer and the agrarian myth versus commercial free market economy. This myth continues today—just listen to members of the agriculture committees in Congress talk about farmers. Consider the role of the marketplace, transportation, machinery, etc. in the evolution of American agriculture.

What were the "good old days" really like? This reference keeps coming up, with revivals and beliefs that things used to be better "back then." Use this question as the first volley to discuss what life was really like. Ask students how many want to go back and live as these settlers did. Continue the same exposé up to the present.

Related Films

"Gone West" This is from Alistair Cooke's *America* series, which dates the material by some 20 years. It describes how the American people filled up the nation east of the Mississippi during the first half of the nineteenth century. It also includes information on the first migrations of settlers to the Pacific, conflicts with Native Americans, and how these encounters altered the cultures of both groups. Finally, it demonstrates the difficulties encountered by pioneers and settlers heading West, which connects nicely with the themes in both the video segment and the textbook.

America Grows Up: Part I This video describes the transition of America from a rural and agricultural nation into an industrialized urban nation. It might not have enough on rural America for some instructors.

"Life in America around 1800" This is from the *Had You Lived Then* series. It focuses on daily life in a rural New England village. It lets students see how life could be tied to events in the general store and town hall. It also illustrates the growing connection to the market economy and democracy.

"The Expanding Nation" From the *American Adventure* series. This video connects the rapid growth of agriculture in the Old Northwest and Old Southwest with the expansion of industry in the antebellum United States. It also points out the geographic expansion west of the Mississippi and how the growth of a transportation network tied the nation together. Too ambitious for one video, but it has its moments.

"The Rural Republic" From the *American Adventure* series. It provides students with a clear picture of the ancient cycles of planting and harvesting as they existed in the rural world of the frontier. It examines social customs and rural order, how settlers formed communities and developed schools, courthouses, and legal order. Furthermore, it covers sexual divisions of labor in traditional America. This content is an excellent match for material in *Liberty, Equality, Power*.

In addition, you may utilize three excellent video indexes. The R. R. Bowker Company publishes two of them:

The Educational Film & Video Locator of the Consortium of College and University Media Centers, two volumes.

The AV Marketplace Film & Video Finder, three volumes, by the National Information Center for Educational Media.

If you want other ideas on how to raise questions about historical films or get your students involved in critiquing popular films based on historical topics, you can turn to two sources. The December 1986 issue of *The Journal of American History* and the December 1988 issue of *The American Historical Review* provide examples of both how historians question filmmaking accuracy and how they review the finished product.

Let the End Be Legitimate: The Supreme Court, The National Government, and the National Economy

Overview

Liberty, Equality, Power in Chapters 8, 9, and 11, as well as this video segment, introduces students to the Supreme Court and the major cases of *Marbury* v. *Madison, McCulloch* v. *Maryland*, and *Gibbons* v. *Ogden*. The textbook raises the question about the role of the Court in society and the idea of judicial review of cases. It also provides students a background about the role of the government in the economy. This debate starts with Hamilton and Jefferson, is carried through Henry Clay and the American System, and the issue of government spending and intervention as applied to canals, tariffs, etc. The debate about the government's role in economic development continues into the Jacksonian period with Jackson versus the Whigs. What is the role of the government in a market economy? Should it stay out entirely, or does it have a responsibility to promote economic development, thus increasing power and equality for all? How this debate applied to banking powers, international relations, and court rulings are all examined by text and video. In addition, the text provides marvelous information in the rest of Chapter 9 on the conversion from agrarianism to industrialism, and how this change affects people. This, of course, has a direct relationship to citizens' views on the government's role in the economy.

Classroom Use of Video Segment

This subject matter all ties into the video segment quite well. You can use this reading material as an introduction, or remind students that nothing occurs in a vacuum. Political issues, social issues, economic issues, and legal decisions are all linked and influence each one another.

You might want to remind students (either on their own or referring them back to earlier chapters in the book) that there was a need for the Commerce Clause and federal regulation of trade. Consider the economic warfare between states under the Articles of Confederation (1781–1787), and students will better understand Chief Justice Marshall's determination that the national government's power over commerce be strong. Also focus on the relationship between the federal power under the Commerce Clause and the regulation of slavery. Students might not understand southerners' insistence that federal power be limited in banking without understanding the implication for slavery. A consideration of South Carolina's paranoia about its slaves might be advantageous here (along the lines of William Freehling's books). You could carry this debate over government power and regulation right up to the present, including evidence where self-interest is cloaked in terms of "states rights."

The Founding Fathers' liberty increased with a limited central government. This part of the textbook hotly debates this idea and the role of government changes. The debate continues today, with arguments over how much the national, state, or local governments should regulate the economy, morality, etc. Have your students start a timeline and trace the roots of current arguments from the earliest days of our constitutional government.

At the most basic level, students can identify how the role of the government changed between 1790 and 1860, and why.

Students should identify the connection between social issues and government action, and the reasons advocated for or against government intervention. Students can tie this examination into the struggle between liberty and power.

Students should do a similar examination for economic issues and examine the myth of laissez-faire.

There is an ongoing struggle for power between the national and state governments. (This struggle can also be traced from Confederation days to current welfare and other reform arguments). Have students think critically about this struggle—is it another example of the struggle between liberty and power? Are the two always mutually exclusive? How do citizens come out the winner, and what promotes equality?

How do students explain the rise of political parties using the debate over liberty and power, and questions about the role of government? Students can trace the development of Federalists, Democratic-Republicans, Whigs, and other parties—and their ideologies—through to the present-day parties. How have the basic appeals and definitions of liberty, equality, and power changed as society changes?

Our government evolved from a deferential representative republican government to a democracy during this time period. But it became a democracy for whom? How much liberty, power, and equality did the people gain, and was this equally divided? Who was left out of the loop, and how did the rest of the citizens and leaders justify this with our Constitutional principles? (Another line of reasoning that students can continue throughout the course).

The video on immigration also applies to this topic.

Liberty, Equality, Power also examines foreign relations as an issue of liberty and power. Using this idea, students can investigate our foreign relations and wars.

How do these events increase or decrease our power and liberty as a nation? What was the intent of the actions on our part?

How does the outcome of our foreign relations increase liberty, equality, or power for the average citizen?

The beginning of Chapter 9 provides a great link between foreign affairs and domestic legislation.

Suggested Classroom Exercises

History of the Supreme Court and the Constitution. This can be connected with background of the Founding Fathers, the Federalist Papers, and their intent for both the Constitution and the Court's role in government. This history could include how the role and the views of the Court vary depending on its composition and the current attitudes in American society. Use the examples of the Taney Court and the Dred Scott decision, of the conservative bastions of the 1920s and the changes in the 1930s, and of the Court up through Warren and Rehnquist.

Use the video to discuss the ongoing struggle between power and liberty, and over who shall exercise both. This discussion can be linked to changing economic ideas and prosperity, to the argument between state versus national powers, or to the question about personal rights and liberties. Another possibility is to consider the issue of personal versus corporate rights, or the public good versus private property rights. All topics are introduced in this video segment.

The role of government, from early republic to the present. Why should the national government be powerful, and do we still need this today? How powerful is too powerful, i.e., when does the exercise of power become an abuse? Trace the extension of regulatory power from these cases to the Interstate Commerce Commission in 1887, the Food & Drug Administration, OSHA, and others today. What is the real issue behind the power to tax or to create and control the money supply? Why is it constitutional to create national banks but not the Federal Reserve, as some groups suggest? When is regulation considered to be for the public good, and how can you make this determination? (Consider *Munn* v. *Illinois* and other cases as an extension).

What is the correct interpretation of the Constitution and its grants of power? What is meant by the "original intent" of the writers of the document and its amendments, and how do you apply that then and now? What is the difference between "strict construction" and a loose interpretation of the Constitution, and why is each important? This question can be used to delve into the issues of judicial review, civil rights legislation, affirmative action, gun control, personal privacy laws (e.g., abortion), and the claim that government should impose religion and morality.

Related Films

John Marshall: Profile in Courage This biography of Marshall and his career is not impartial but defends him and his decisions against any charges of partisanship. However, it does accurately portray his determination to strengthen national power and the Constitution vis-a-vis the states and thus help the nation survive.

Equal Justice under Law: Marbury v. Madison This is the first video in the series the students view for this segment. This video covers the Marshall Court's affirming the right of judicial review by the Supreme Court. The dramatization reminds everyone that law evolves from real-life events.

In addition, you can make use of three excellent video indexes. The R. R. Bowker Company publishes two of them:

> *The Educational Film & Video Locator of the Consortium of College and University Media Centers*, two volumes.
> *The AV Marketplace Film and Video Finder*, three volumes, by the National Information Center for Educational Media.

If you want other ideas on how to raise questions about historical films and how to get your students involved in critiquing popular films based on historical topics, you can turn to two sources. The December 1986 issue of *The Journal of American History* and the December 1988 issue of *The American Historical Review* provide examples of how historians question filmmaking accuracy and how they review the finished product.

Art, Romanticism, and Culture: Connections East and West

Overview

Chapters 10 and 12 take a close look at the development of American popular culture. The author includes a look at literature, the rise of "sentimentality" in writing, and the fine arts. He establishes for the students the unique relationship between the wilderness frontier and American civilization. This relationship was understood (even overemphasized) by generations of artists and writers. The wilderness provides the difference between what is European or American, between Old World and New. The author also introduces the artists' belief in the morality and godliness of nature and explains that some persons were already questioning whether humans and nature could coexist but were sure that humanity could learn lessons from nature if it paid attention. Note the role of Niagara Falls in the East as an example. The textbook, combined with this video segment, provides a clear basis for eastern art and its appreciation of the West.

Classroom Use of Video Segment

Stress to your students the connection between the ideas of artists and what they saw (or expected to see) in the West. Are the artists' assumptions correct? Do they reinforce the ideas held by Cole and easterners about the connection between nature and Native Americans, that those who live closest to nature learn the most from it?

You might want to provide more information about Thomas Cole and the Hudson River school of painting. Slides of Cole's work, along with that of Inness or Bingham would also help.

The United States develops its own culture—literature, art forms, entertainment. Each of these reflect the democratic impulse of the nation in some way.

What causes the development of popular literature, and how does it reflect or even promote the themes of liberty and equality?

Changes in popular sports emerge in the cities—are they a sign of power shifts or greater liberty?

How does the evolution of America's artists reflect the ideas of liberty, of religion and morality, and of the belief in America's unique place in the world?

Even the shifts in the educational system, or the promotion of widespread education, reflect a belief that this will give power and equality to some citizens. How is this so?

Suggested Classroom Exercises

You may use this video to raise environmental issues; how environmentally conscious have Americans been throughout history? What is the effect of "civilization" on nature? The pictures of Bodner along the Missouri River and out West make a nice counterplay to images of strip mining, deforestation, etc. Can nature and industry coexist without injuring each other? George Inness suggests they can; events in Oregon and elsewhere argue otherwise.

Examine cultural exchanges and diversity in the American past. You can also link the past to the present here. What has the effect of disease been on other cultures we have encountered? (Both in the past and currently.) This consideration ties into examination of the treatment of Native Americans, their poverty, and policies towards them, from colonial times through the present.

This video could be used as part of an examination of Native Americans and their culture.

Also appropriate is a discussion of popular myths and images of the American West, both from the eyes of easterners and from Europe.

Related Films

Views of a Vanishing Frontier This video concentrates on the travels of Karl Bodner, one of the three artists examined in the video segment. In many ways it is an extended version of what the segment does, because it documents their travels from 1832 to 1833 up the Missouri River, recreates the lives of Native Americans before they are struck down with white diseases, and views the frontier before it is assaulted environmentally. The details of Native American dress and ceremonies are striking.

Suggestions for Instructional Use of Video Segments

corresponding to Chapters 13–19

Constitutional Principles and Race Relations: The Beginning

Overview

This video segment addresses the question of the compromises on slavery that emerged in discussions during the Constitutional Convention. It also speaks to the relation of these compromises to the practical but paradoxical determination among the men gathered in Philadelphia to protect individual liberty, security, and property while at the same time establishing a government that could not be torn apart by faction or passion. Bill Moyers, in this video originally produced for the bicentennial of the Constitutional Convention, talks with three historians, Michael Kammen of Cornell University, Forrest McDonald of the University of Alabama, and Olive Taylor of Howard University.

In the initial segment, Moyers questions Forrest McDonald on the value systems of the Founding Fathers vis-à-vis their willingness to compromise on the slavery question in order to succeed in creating a national government that could govern effectively. McDonald notes that protecting liberty was of primary importance to the framers and that the protection of liberties could not occur without union. To have a union, he argues, the framers had to recognize practical realities. He points to the three-fifths compromise as a primary example.

The second part of this segment focuses on Moyers's interview with Olive Taylor, whose most recent scholarly work examines Chief Justice of the Supreme Court John Marshall, "Mr. Constitution." She explains that her interest in Justice Marshall emanated from his insistence on protecting property rights during his tenure on the Court. As a result of this determination and his interest in promoting the sovereignty of the national government, Marshall's decisions even overrode state efforts to loosen the bonds of slavery. To Moyers's question regarding Marshall's racial views, Taylor iterates that the chief justice's position on the issue of slavery in the states had nothing to do with race hatred. She believes that he saw the United States as a "beacon for white people" and a symbol for the realization (ironically) of man's desire for freedom and self-determination. To John Marshall and many like him, blacks simply had no place in this world view.

Although highly critical of the Founding Fathers and shapers of history like John Marshall, Taylor recognizes that the reality of nineteenth-century belief in the sanctity of property and the heritage of Anglo-Saxon jurisprudence meant that these men were not going to tamper with the institution of slavery. She uses the carving of the nation's capital out of two slave states to illustrate their willingness to compromise on the issue of slavery, in part to pacify southerners concerned about antislavery agitation in New York and Pennsylvania and to win southern support for Alexander Hamilton's economic policy.

Despite such practical, if unfortunate, considerations, Taylor admits that the genius of the document is that it can be changed and that the Constitution has a positive meaning for most blacks. Although it took many years, "the moral arm of the universe" did bend toward justice—as evidenced in the Constitution's ability to finally bring justice to the doorstep of all Americans, regardless of race. The Constitution lives, she concludes, and it works.

In the video segment's final part, Moyers interviews Michael Kammen. Moyers relates Carl Sandburg's statement that Lincoln said yes to the Constitution when it could be a help and no when it became a hindrance. Kammen contends that the Constitution is a living document that fortunately allows the kind of flexibility that Lincoln demonstrated. During the Civil War, America's single greatest crisis as a people, the question "Is the Constitution adequate to a crisis like this?" constantly arose. The outcome proved it was. It also revealed that the Constitution could serve as a means to an end—the preservation of our individual rights, security, and cohesion of a nation.

Classroom Use of Video Segment

First list and then discuss the values involved in the treatment of the issue of slavery at the Constitutional Convention.

Have your students reflect on John Marshall's interpretation of the Constitution as it relates to the questions of African Americans and the issues of liberty, equality, and power.

The video segment refers to the "genius" of the Constitution. Have your class analyze this claim, in particular, as related to race relations.

Discuss how Abraham Lincoln reflected that "genius" in his presidency.

Concluding Questions

Although Chief Justice John Marshall adhered to the principle of the sanctity of property rights that allowed the institution of slavery to remain viable, he also asserted the supremacy of the national government over the states in his decisions. How did the precedents set in Marshall's decisions ultimately serve the purposes of those who opposed slavery?

In terms of the institution of slavery and black civil rights, how did the "moral arm of justice" bend during the decade preceding the Civil War and through the Reconstruction era? What made this possible at that time and again some one hundred years later?

"Free Soil" advocates denounced the Dred Scott decision as a "gross perversion" of the Constitution, while southerners gloated that "Southern opinion upon the subject of Southern slavery . . . is now the supreme law of the land." What constitutional debate in the post–Mexican War era did these opposing positions reflect? What did this dispute say about the document the framers of the Constitution produced?

Carl Sandburg said that Abraham Lincoln said yes to the Constitution when it was a help and no when it was a hindrance. How is Lincoln's practical genius in using the Constitution reflected in his actions in the events immediately preceding the outbreak of the Civil War and in decisions he made during the war and as the war drew to a close?

Video to Text Issues

Did Americans not see the hypocrisy and paradox inherent in the compromises on the issue of slavery in the Constitution? Explain.

If the framers of the Constitution and subsequent eras could compromise on the issue of slavery, why was this not possible in the decade preceding the Civil War?

Suggested Classroom Exercises

Since the constitutional debates that preceded the Civil War are among the most important in American history, this video segment and the one that follows offer an excellent launching point for an examination of constitutional issues reflected in the post–Mexican War debate over slavery in the territory acquired from Mexico, such as the:

- appearance of a Free Soil party
- forging of the Compromise of 1850
- Lincoln-Douglas debates
- Kansas crisis
- Dred Scott and other Supreme Court decisions in the period
- position of Lincoln's assumption on the nature of the southern rebellion and the president's role in responding to it, his decision to issue the Emancipation Proclamation, his conduct of the war, and his view of reconstructing the South

- debates between Congress and the presidents (Lincoln and Johnson) on plans of Reconstruction
- passage of civil rights legislation during the Reconstruction period and the de facto abrogation of black civil rights by the end of the nineteenth century

The subject of conflicting interpretations of the Constitution relating to a variety of issues today is a relevant topic that students can easily discuss and for which they can find many current examples. [Debates over gun control, affirmative action, the extent of the federal government's obligation to provide for the general welfare, a citizen's privacy versus the government's responsibility to regulate (e.g., abortion), and legislation that abridges individual liberty for the common good (prohibitions against smoking in public places, for example).

These video segments also can be used as a basis for critical thinking exercises that demand the analysis of historical data to reach an appropriate conclusion or to explain a decision or an action.

To address the Constitutional issues inherent in the Dred Scott decision and the significance of the context in which the justices heard the case, distribute (1) the basic elements of the arguments in Taney's opinion, (2) a descriptive composite of each justice sitting on the Supreme Court at the time the Dred Scott case reached the court, and (3) a description of the context in which the decision was handed down—controversial events that had preceded the hearing of the case. Ask students to draw conclusions based on an analysis of this data and to explain how this decision was a product of its time, much as the compromises on slavery in the Constitutional Convention reflected the pressure of the job at hand and the times in which the framers lived.

An analysis of events in the aftermath of the Mexican War that led to the Kansas crisis offers the opportunity to understand how the effort to compromise generated more problems than it solved.

An examination of the behavior of southern secessionists, northern abolitionists, and Radical Republicans reflects the consequences of a refusal to compromise on Constitutional principles or to accept the legitimacy of the Constitution in a crisis (in the case of the "Fire Eaters" and the William Lloyd Garrison brand of abolitionism).

Related Films

The Sellin' of Jamie Thomas, Parts 1 and 2 A dramatization of the sale of a slave family, their escape to freedom, and the threat of bounty hunters to that freedom.

Digging for Slaves: The Excavation of American Slave Sites An examination of three slave quarter excavations at eighteenth-century sites at Monticello, Williamsburg, and Middleburg Plantation that contribute to our knowledge of the reality of slavery.

In Search of the Dream: Origins A review of the origins of slavery in seventeenth-century Virginia, the impact of the institution on African Americans, and the African cultural heritage still reflected in American life.

Uncle Tom's Cabin A description of the impact of Harriet Beecher Stowe's novel and the popularity of the play that was produced across the United States in the post–Civil War period, concluding with an abridged dramatic production of the play.

Frederick Douglass: The Lesson of the Hour (I)

Overview

In this final video segment on Volume I, actor Fred Morsell dramatizes the last and most important speech delivered by Frederick Douglass. Titled "The Lesson of the Hour," this speech reflects the horror and disgust that famed runaway slave and abolitionist leader Douglass felt as southern whites used lynchings and economic, political, and social degradation to return blacks to a virtual enslaved condition in the late nineteenth century. He eloquently appeals to Americans to uphold the basic principles on which their nation was built. Only then, he argues, can justice prevail for all the people. Chapter 18 in *Liberty, Equality, Power* provides a very nice complement to this video segment. You might wish to have your students read the chapter and then follow with Douglass's speech at the end of class or have the students view it on their own after reading the chapter and essay.

Classroom Use of Video Segment

Describe and analyze Douglass's solutions to the "Negro problem."

According to Morsell's depiction of Douglass, describe Douglass's frame of mind when he wrote and delivered this speech.

Concluding Questions

To what post–Civil War outrages against blacks was Douglass referring, and what effect did these outrages have on his perception of the importance of this speech? Did his speech accomplish what he had hoped?

Suggested Classroom Exercises

An analysis of how and why, after a Civil War and traumatic postwar period, African Americans failed to experience the full protection of their rights under the Constitution.

For Text to Video Issues and Related Films: see previous video segment.